F# for Machine Learning Essentials

Get up and running with machine learning with F# in a fun and functional way

Sudipta Mukherjee

[PACKT] PUBLISHING open source community experience distilled

BIRMINGHAM - MUMBAI

F# for Machine Learning Essentials

First published: February 2016

Production reference: 1190216

Published by Packt Publishing Ltd.
Livery Place
35 Livery Street
Birmingham B3 2PB, UK.

ISBN 978-1-78398-934-8

www.packtpub.com

Credits

Author
Sudipta Mukherjee

Reviewers
Alena Hall
David Stephens

Commissioning Editor
Ashwin Nair

Acquisition Editors
Harsha Bharwani
Larissa Pinto

Content Development Editor
Athira Laji

Technical Editor
Ryan Kochery

Copy Editor
Alpha Singh

Project Coordinator
Bijal Patel

Proofreader
Safis Editing

Indexer
Rekha Nair

Graphics
Abhinash Sahu

Production Coordinator
Aparna Bhagat

Cover Work
Aparna Bhagat

Foreword

Machine Learning (ML) is one of the most impactful technologies of the last 10 years, fueled by the exponential growth of electronic data about people and their interaction with the world and each other, as well as the availability of massive computing power to extract patterns from data. Applications of ML are already affecting all of us in everyday life, whether it's face recognition in modern cameras, personalized web or product searches, or even the detection of road sign patterns in modern cars. Machine learning is a set of algorithms that learn prediction programs from past data in order to use them for future predictions—whether the prediction programs are represented as decision trees, as neural networks, or via nearest-neighbor functions.

Another influential development in computer science is the invention of F#. Less than 10 years ago, functional programming was a more of an academic endeavor than a style of programming and software development used in production systems. The development of F# since 2005 changed this forever. With F#, programmers are not only able to benefit from type inference and easy parallelization of workflows, but they also get the runtime performance that they are used to from programming in other .NET languages, such as C#. I personally witnessed this transformation at Microsoft Research and saw how data-intensive applications could be written much more safely in less than 100 lines of F# code compared to thousands of lines of C# code.

A critically important ingredient of ML is data; it's the lifeblood of any ML algorithm. Parsing, cleaning, and visualizing data is the basis of any successful ML application and constitutes the majority of the time that practitioners spend in making machine learning systems work. F# proves to be the perfect bridge between data processing and analysis, with ML on one hand and the ability to invent new ML algorithms on the other hand.

In this book, Sudipta Mukherjee introduces the reader to the basics of machine learning, ranging from supervised methods, such as classification learning and regression, to unsupervised methods, such as K-means clustering. Sudipta focuses on the applied aspects of machine learning and develops all algorithms in F#, both natively as well as by integrating with .NET libraries such as WekaSharp, Accord.Net and Math.Net. He covers a wide range of algorithms for classification and regression learning and also explores more novel ML concepts, such as anomaly detection. The book is enriched with directly applicable source code examples, and the reader will enjoy learning about modern machine learning algorithms through the numerous examples provided.

Dr. Ralf Herbrich

Director of Machine Learning Science at Amazon

About the Author

Sudipta Mukherjee was born in Kolkata and migrated to Bangalore. He is an electronics engineer by education and a computer engineer/scientist by profession and passion. He graduated in 2004 with a degree in electronics and communication engineering.

He has a keen interest in data structure, algorithms, text processing, natural language processing tools development, programming languages, and machine learning at large. His first book on *Data Structure using C* has been received quite well. Parts of the book can be read on Google Books at `http://goo.gl/pttSh`. The book was also translated into simplified Chinese, available from Amazon.cn at `http://goo.gl/lc536`. This is Sudipta's second book with Packt Publishing. His first book, *.NET 4.0 Generics* (`http://goo.gl/MN18ce`), was also received very well. During the last few years, he has been hooked to the functional programming style. His book on functional programming, *Thinking in LINQ* (`http://goo.gl/hm0lNF`), was released last year. Last year, he also gave a talk at `@FuConf` based on his LINQ book (`https://goo.gl/umdxIX`). He lives in Bangalore with his wife and son.

Sudipta can be reached via e-mail at `sudipto80@yahoo.com` and via Twitter at `@samthecoder`.

Acknowledgments

First, I want to thank Dr. Don Syme (`@dsyme`) and everyone in the product team who brought F# to the world and made a fantastic integration with Visual Studio. I also want to thank Professor Andrew Ng (`@AndrewYNg`). I first learned about machine learning from his MOOC on machine learning at Coursera (`https://www.coursera.org/learn/machine-learning`).

This book couldn't have seen the light of day without a few people: my acquisition editor, Ms. Harsha Bharwani, who persuaded me to work on this book; and my development editor, Ms. Athira Laji, who tolerated many delays in the delivery schedule but kept the bar high and got me going. She is one of the most compassionate development editors I have ever worked with. Thank you mam! I have been fortunate to have a couple of very educated reviewers on board: Mr. David Stephens (the PM of the F# programming language) (`@NumberByColors`) and Ms. Alena Dzenisenka (`@lenadroid`). The book uses several open source frameworks and F#. So, thanks to all the people who have contributed to these projects. I also want to say a huge thank you to Dr. Ralf Herbrich (`@rherbrich`), the director of machine learning science at Amazon, Berlin, for kindly writing a foreword for the book.

Last but not least, I must say that I am very fortunate to have a very loving family, who always stood by me whenever I needed support. My wife, Mou, made sure that I had enough time to write the chapters. We couldn't go out on weekends. I promise to make up for all the missed family time. Thank you sweetheart! My son, Sohan, has been my inspiration. His enthusiasm makes me feel happy. Love you son. I hope when he grows up, machine learning will be more mainstream and will have become far more commonplace in the programming ecosystem than it is now. My dad, Subrata, always inspired me to learn more about mathematics. I realized how important mathematics is in programming while writing this book. My mom, Dipali, taught me mathematics in my early years and what I know today about mathematics is deeply rooted in her teachings. I love you all!

I am thankful to God for giving me the strength to dream big and fight my nightmares.

About the Reviewers

Alena Hall is an experienced Solution Architect proficient in distributed cloud programming, real-time system modeling, higher load and performance, big data analysis, data science, functional programming, and machine learning. She is a speaker at international conferences and a member of the F# Board of Trustees.

David Stephens is the program manager for Visual F# at Microsoft. He's responsible for representing the needs of F# developers within Microsoft, managing the development of new features, and evangelizing F#. Prior to joining the .NET team, David worked on tools for Apache Cordova, the F12 developer tools in Microsoft Edge, TypeScript, and .NET Native. He has a bachelor's degree in computer science and mathematics from the Raikes School of Computer Science and Management at the University of Nebraska in Lincoln, Nebraska, USA.

Table of Contents

Preface

Machine learning (ML) is more prevalent now than ever before. Every day a lot of data is being generated. Machine learning algorithms perform heavy duty number crunching to improve our lives every day. The following image captures the major tasks that machine learning algorithms perform. These are the classes or types of problems that ML algorithms solve.

Our lives are more and more driven by the output of these ML algorithms than we care to admit. Let me walk you through the image once:

- Computers everywhere: Now your smartphone can beat a vintage supercomputer, and computer are everywhere: in your phone, camera, car, microwave, and so on.
- Clustering: Clustering is the task of identifying groups of items from a given list that seem to be similar to the others in the group. Clustering has many diverse uses. However, it is heavily used in market segment analysis to identify different categories of customers.

- Classification: This is the ML algorithm that works hard to keep your spam e-mails away from your priority inbox. The same algorithm can be used to identify objects from images or videos and surprisingly, the same algorithm can be used to predict whether a patient has cancer or not. Generally, a lot of data is provided to the algorithm, from which it learns. That's why this set of algorithms is sometime referred to as supervised learning algorithms, and this constitutes the vast majority of machine learning algorithms.
- Predictions: There are several ML algorithms that perform predictions for several situations that are important in life. For example, there are predictors that predict fuel price in the near future. This family of algorithms is known as regressions.
- Anomaly detection: Anomaly, as the name suggests, relates to items that have attributes that are not similar to normal ones. Anomaly detection algorithms use statistical methods to find out the anomalous items from a given list automatically. This is an example of unsupervised learning. Anomaly detection has several diverse uses, such as finding faulty items in factories to finding intruders on a video stream coming from a surveillance camera, and so on.
- Recommendations: Every time you visit Amazon and rate a product, the site recommends some items to you. Under the hood is a clever machine learning algorithm in action called collaborative filtering, which takes cues from other users purchasing similar items as you are. Recommender systems are a very active research topic now and several other algorithms are being considered.
- Sentiment analysis: Whenever a product hits the market, the company that brought it into the market wants to know how the market is reacting towards it. Is it positive or negative? Sentiment analysis techniques help to identify these reactions. Also, in review websites, people post several comments, and the website might be interested in publishing a generalized positive or negative rating for the item under review. Here, sentiment analysis techniques can be quite helpful.
- Information retrieval: Whenever you hit the search button on your favorite search engine, a plethora of information retrieval algorithms are used under the hood. These algorithms are also used in the content-based filtering that is used in recommender systems.

Now that you have a top-level idea of what ML algorithms can do for you, let's see why F# is the perfect fit for the implementations. Here are my reasons for using F# to implement machine learning algorithms:

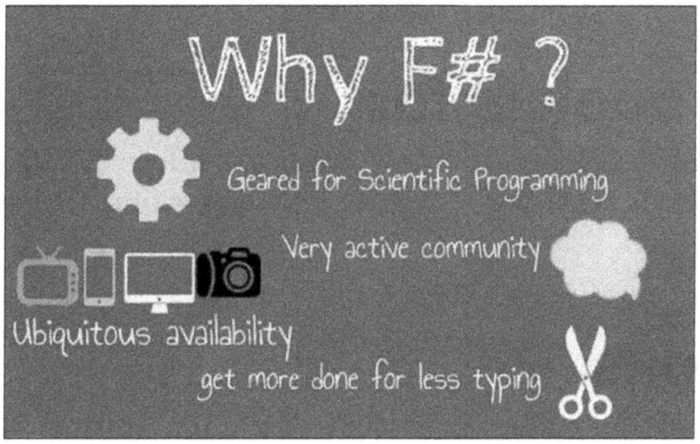

What this book covers

Chapter 1, Introduction to Machine Learning, introduces machine learning concepts.

Chapter 2, Linear Regression, introduces and implements several linear regression models using F#.

Chapter 3, Classification Techniques, introduces classification as a formal problem and then solves some use cases using F#.

Chapter 4, Information Retrieval, provides implementations of several information retrieval distance metrics that can be useful in several situations.

Chapter 5, Collaborative Filtering, explains the workhorse algorithm for recommender systems, provides an implementation using F#, and then shows how to evaluate such a system.

Chapter 6, Sentiment Analysis, explains sentiment analysis and after positioning it as a formal problem statement, solves it using several state-of-the-art algorithms.

Chapter 7, Anomaly Detection, explains and poses the anomaly detection problem statement and then gives several algorithms and their implementation in F#.

What you need for this book

You will need Visual Studio 2010 or above and a good internet connection because some of the plotting APIs used here rely on connectivity.

Who this book is for

If you are a C# or F# developer who now wants to explore the area of machine learning, then this book is for you. No prior knowledge of machine learning is assumed.

Conventions

In this book, you will find a number of styles of text that distinguish between different kinds of information. Here are some examples of these styles, and an explanation of their meaning.

Code words in text, database table names, folder names, filenames, file extensions, pathnames, dummy URLs, user input, and Twitter handles are shown as follows: "For example, `able` has a positive polarity of `0.125` and `unable` has a negative polarity of `0.75`."

A block of code is set as follows:

```
let calculateSO (docs:string list list)(words:string list)=
    let mutable res  = 0.0
    for i in 0 .. docs.Length - 1 do
        for j in 0 .. docs.[i].Length - 1    do
            for pw in words do
                 res <- res + pmi docs docs.[i].[j] pw
    res
```

When we wish to draw your attention to a particular part of a code block, the relevant lines or items are set in bold:

```
Calling this function is simple as shown below.
//The above rating matrix is represented as (float list)list in F#
let ratings = [[4.;0.;5.;5.];[4.;2.;1.;0.];[3.;0.;2.;4.];[4.;4.;0.;0.]
;[2.;1.;3.;5.]]
//Finding the predicted rating for user 1 for item 2
let p12 = Predictu  ratings  0 1
```

Any command-line input or output is written as follows:

```
if d1 = 0.0 || d2 = 0.0 then 0.0 else num  / ((sqrt d1) * (sqrt d2 ))
```

New terms and **important words** are shown in bold. Words that you see on the screen, in menus or dialog boxes for example, appear in the text like this: "Navigate to **user id** and then on **item id**."

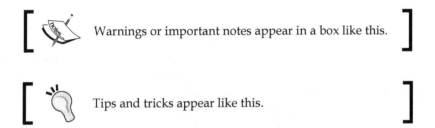

[Warnings or important notes appear in a box like this.]

[Tips and tricks appear like this.]

Reader feedback

Feedback from our readers is always welcome. Let us know what you think about this book—what you liked or may have disliked. Reader feedback is important for us to develop titles that you really get the most out of.

To send us general feedback, simply send an e-mail to `feedback@packtpub.com`, and mention the book title via the subject of your message.

If there is a topic that you have expertise in and you are interested in either writing or contributing to a book, see our author guide on `www.packtpub.com/authors`.

Customer support

Now that you are the proud owner of a Packt book, we have a number of things to help you to get the most from your purchase.

Downloading the example code

You can download the example code files from `https://github.com/sudipto80/fsharpforml`. You can also visit `www.twitter.com/fsharpforml` for more updates on the F#.

Downloading the color images of this book

We also provide you with a PDF file that has color images of the screenshots/diagrams used in this book. The color images will help you better understand the changes in the output. You can download this file from `https://www.packtpub.com/sites/default/files/downloads/FForMachineLearning_ColorImages.pdf`.

Errata

Although we have taken every care to ensure the accuracy of our content, mistakes do happen. If you find a mistake in one of our books—maybe a mistake in the text or the code—we would be grateful if you could report this to us. By doing so, you can save other readers from frustration and help us improve subsequent versions of this book. If you find any errata, please report them by visiting `http://www.packtpub.com/submit-errata`, selecting your book, clicking on the **Errata Submission Form** link, and entering the details of your errata. Once your errata are verified, your submission will be accepted and the errata will be uploaded to our website or added to any list of existing errata under the Errata section of that title.

To view the previously submitted errata, go to `https://www.packtpub.com/books/content/support` and enter the name of the book in the search field. The required information will appear under the **Errata** section.

Piracy

Piracy of copyrighted material on the Internet is an ongoing problem across all media. At Packt, we take the protection of our copyright and licenses very seriously. If you come across any illegal copies of our works in any form on the Internet, please provide us with the location address or website name immediately so that we can pursue a remedy.

Please contact us at `copyright@packtpub.com` with a link to the suspected pirated material.

We appreciate your help in protecting our authors and our ability to bring you valuable content.

Questions

If you have a problem with any aspect of this book, you can contact us at `questions@packtpub.com`, and we will do our best to address the problem.

1
Introduction to Machine Learning

"To learn is to discover patterns."

You have been using products that employ machine learning, but maybe you've never realized that the systems or programs that you have been using, use **machine learning** under the hood. Most of what machine learning does today is inspired by sci-fi movies. Machine learning scientists and researchers are on a perpetual quest to make the gap between the sci-fi movies and the reality disappear. Learning about machine learning algorithms can be fun.

This is going to be a very practical book about machine learning. Throughout the book I will be using several machine learning frameworks adopted by the industry. So I will cut the theory of machine learning short and will get away with just enough to implement it. My objective in this chapter is to get you excited about machine learning by showing how you can use these techniques to solve real world problems.

Objective

After reading this chapter, you will be able to understand the different terminologies used in machine learning and the process of performing machine learning activities. Also, you will be able to look at a problem statement and immediately identify which problem domain the problem belongs to; whether it is a classification or a regression problem, and such. You will find connections between seemingly disparate sets of problems. You will also find basic intuition behind some of the major algorithms used in machine learning today. Finally, I wrap up this chapter with a motivating example of identifying hand written digits using a supervised learning algorithm. This is analogous to your `Hello world` program.

Getting in touch

I have created the following Twitter account for you (my dear reader) to get in touch with me. If you want to ask a question, post errata, or just have a suggestion, tag this twitter ID and I will surely get back as soon as I can.

```
https://twitter.com/fsharpforml
```

I will post contents here that will augment the content in the book.

Different areas where machine learning is being used

The preceding image shows some of the areas where machine learning techniques are used extensively. In this book, you will learn about most of these usages.

Machines learn almost the same way as we humans do. We learn in three different ways.

As kids our parents taught us the alphabets and thus we can distinguish between the A's and H's. The same is true with machines. Machines are also taught the same way to recognize characters. This is known as **supervised learning**.

While growing up, we taught ourselves the differences between the teddy bear toy and an actual bear. This is known as **unsupervised learning**, because there is no supervision required in the process of the learning. The main type of unsupervised learning is called **clustering**; that's the art of finding groups in unlabeled datasets. Clustering has several applications, one of them being customer base segmentation.

Remember those days when you first learnt how to take the stairs? You probably fell many times before successfully taking the stairs. However, each time you fell, you learnt something useful that helped you later. So your learning got re-enforced every time you fell. This process is known as **reinforcement learning**. Ever saw those funky robots crawling uneven terrains like humans. That's the result of re-enforcement learning. This is a very active topic of research.

Whenever you shop online at Amazon or on other sites, the site recommends back to you other stuff that you might be interested in. This is done by a set of algorithms known as **recommender systems**.

Machine learning is very heavily used to determine whether suspicious credit card transactions are fraudulent or not. The technique used is popularly known as **anomaly detection**. Anomaly detection works on the assumption that most of the entries are proper and that the entry that is far (also called an outlier) from the other entries is probably fraudulent.

In the coming decade, machine learning is going to be very commonplace and it's about time to democratize the machine learning techniques. In the next few sections, I will give you a few examples where these different types of machine learning algorithms are used to solve several problems.

Why use F#?

F# is an open source, functional-first, general purpose programming language and is particularly suitable for developing mathematical models that are an integral part of machine learning algorithm development.

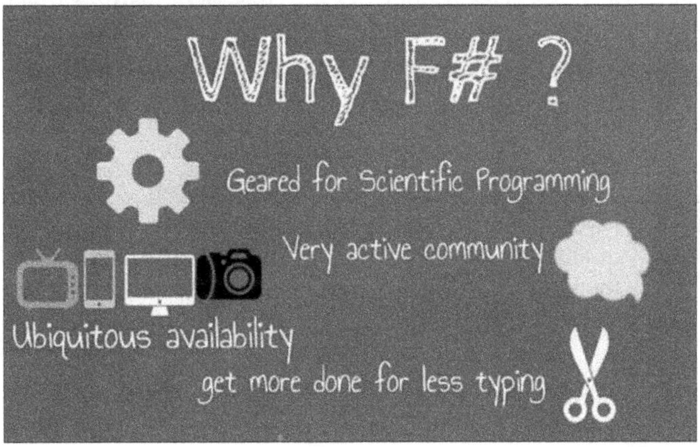

Code written in F# is generally very expressive and is close to its actual algorithm description. That's why you shall see more and more mathematically inclined domains adopting F#.

At every stage of a machine learning activity, F# has a feature or an API to help. Following are the major steps in a machine learning activity:

Major step in machine learning activity	How F# can help
Data Acquisition	F# type providers are great at it. (Refer to `http://blogs.msdn.com/b/dsyme/archive/2013/01/30/twelve-type-providers-in-pictures.aspx`) F# can help you get the data from the following resources using F# type providers: • Databases (SQL Server and such) • XML • CSV • JSON • World Bank • Cloud Storages • Hive
Data Scrubbing/ Data Cleansing	F# list comprehensions are perfect for this task. Deedle (`http://bluemountaincapital.github.io/Deedle/`) is an API written in F#, primarily for exploratory data analysis. This framework also has lot of features that can help in the data cleansing phase.
Learning the Model	WekaSharp is an F# wrapper on top of Weka to help with machine learning tasks such as regression, clustering, and so on. Accord.NET is a massive framework for performing a very diverse set of machine learning.
Data Visualization	F# charts are very interactive and intuitive to easily generate high quality charts. Also, there are several APIs, such as FsPlot, that take the pain of conforming to standards when it comes to plugging data to visualization.

F# has a way to name a variable the way you want if you wrap it with double back quotes like— "my variable". This feature can make the code much more readable.

Supervised machine learning

Supervised machine learning algorithms are mostly broadly classified into two major categories: **classification** and **regression**.

Supervised machine learning algorithms work with labeled datasets. This means that the algorithm takes a lot of labeled data sets, where the data represents the instance and the label represents the class of the data. Sometimes these labels are finite in number and sometimes they are continuous numbers. When the labels belong to a finite set, then the problem of identifying the label of an unknown/new instance is known as a **classification problem**. On the other hand, if the label is a continuous number, then the problem of finding the continuous value for a new instance is known as a **regression problem**. Given a set of records for cancer patients, with test results and labels (*B* for benign and *M* for malignant) predicting whether a new patient's case is B or M, is a classification problem. On the other hand, predicting the price of a house, given the area in square feet and the number of bedrooms in the house, is an example of a regression problem.

I found the following analogy to geometry very useful when thinking about these algorithms.

Let's say you have two points in 2D. You can calculate the Euclidean distance between those two and if that distance is small, you can conclude that those points are close to each other. In other words, if those two points represent two cities in a country, you might conclude that they are in the same district.

Now if you extrapolate this theory to the N dimension, you can immediately see that any measurement can be represented as a point with the N dimension or as a vector of size N and a label can be associated with it. Then an algorithm can be deployed to learn the associativity or the pattern, and thus it learns to predict the label for an unseen/unknown/new instance represented in the similar format.

Training and test dataset/corpus

The phase when an algorithm runs over a labeled data set is known as training, and the labeled data is known as training dataset. Sometimes it is loosely referred to as **training corpus**. Later in the process, the algorithm must be tested with similar un-labeled datasets or for which the label is hidden from the algorithm. This dataset is known as **test dataset** or **test corpus**. Typically, an 80-20 split is used to generate the training and test set from a randomly shuffled labeled data set. This means that 80% of the randomly shuffled labeled data is generally treated as **training data** and the remaining 20% as **test data**.

Some motivating real life examples of supervised learning

Supervised learning algorithms have several applications. Following are some of those. This is by no means a comprehensive list, but it is indicative.

- Classification
    - Spam filtering in your mailbox
    - Cancer prediction from the previous patient records
    - Identifying objects in images/videos
    - Identifying flowers from measurements
    - Identifying hand written digits on cheques
    - Predicting whether there will be a traffic jam in a city
    - Making recommendations to the users based on their and similar user's preferences
- Regression
    - Predicting the price of houses based on several features, such as the number of bedrooms in the house
    - Finding cause-effect relationships between several variables
- Supervised learning algorithms
    - Nearest Neighbor algorithm
    - Support Vector Machine
    - Decision Tree
    - Linear Regression
    - Logistic Regression
    - Naïve Bayes Classifier
    - Neural Networks
    - Recommender systems algorithms
    - Anomaly Detection
    - Sentiment Analysis

In the next few sections, I will walk you through the overview of a few of these algorithms and their mathematical basis. However, we will get away with as minimal math as possible, since the objective of the book is to help you use machine learning in the real settings.

Nearest Neighbour algorithm (a.k.a k-NN algorithm)

As the name suggests, **k-Nearest Neighbor** is an algorithm that works on the distance between two projected points. It relies on the distance of k-nearest neighbors (thus the name) to determine the class/category of the unknown/new test data.

As the name suggests the nearest neighbor algorithm relies on the distance of two data points projected in N-Dimensional space. Let's take a popular example where the k-NN can be used to determine the class. The dataset `https://archive.ics.uci.edu/ml/machine-learning-databases/breast-cancer-wisconsin/wdbc.data` stores data about several patients who were either unfortunate and diagnosed as "Malignant" cases (which are represented as *M* in the dataset), or were fortunate and diagnosed as "Benign" (non-harmful/non-cancerous) cases (which are represented as *B* in the dataset). If you want to understand what all the other fields mean, take a look at `https://archive.ics.uci.edu/ml/machine-learning-databases/breast-cancer-wisconsin/wdbc.names`.

Now the question is, given a new entry with all the other records except the tag M or B, can we predict that? In ML terminology, this value "M" or "B" is sometimes referred to as "class tag" or just "class". The task of a classification algorithm is to determine this class for a new data point. K-NN does this in the following way: it measures the distance from the given data to all the training data and then takes into consideration the classes for only the k-nearest neighbors to determine the class of the new entry. So for the current case, if more than 50% of the k-nearest neighbors is of class "B", then k-NN will conclude that the new entry is of type "B".

Distance metrics

The distance metric used is generally Euclidean, that you learnt in high school. For example, given two points in 3D.

$$d(p,q)=\sqrt{(p_1-q_1)^2+(p_2-q_2)^2+(p_3-q_3)^2}$$

In this preceding example, p_1 and q_1 denote their values in the X axis, p_2 and q_2 denote their values in the Y axis, and p_3 and q_3 denote their values in the z axis.

Extrapolating this, we get the following formula for calculating the distance in N dimension:

$$d(\mathbf{p},\mathbf{q}) = d(\mathbf{q},\mathbf{p}) = \sqrt{(q_1 - p_1)^2 + (q_2 - p_2)^2 + \cdots + (q_n - p_n)^2}$$
$$= \sqrt{\sum_{i=1}^{n} (q_i - p_i)^2}$$

Thus, after calculating the distance from all the training set data, we can create a list of tuples with the distance and the class, as follows. This list is made for the sake of demonstration. This is not calculated from the actual data.

Distance from test/new data	Class/Tag/Category
0.34235	B
0.45343	B
1.34233	B
6.23433	M
66.3435	M

Let's assume that k is set to be 4. Now for each k, we take into consideration the class. So for the first three entries, we found that the class is B and for the last one, it is M. Since the number of B's is more than the number of M's, k-NN will conclude that the new patient's data is of type B.

Decision tree algorithms

Have you ever played the game where you had to guess about a thing that your friend had been thinking about by asking questions? And you were allowed to guess only a certain number of times and had to get back to your friend with your answer about what he/she could probably be thinking about.

The strategy to guess the correct answer is to start asking questions that segregate the possible answer space as evenly as possible. For example, if your friend told you that he/she had imagined about something, then probably the first question you would like to ask him/her is that whether he/she is thinking about an animal or a thing. That would broadly classify the answer space and then later you can ask more direct/specific questions based on the answers previously provided by your friend.

Decision tree is a set of classification algorithm that uses this approach to determine the class of an unknown entry. As the name suggests, a decision tree is a tree where the nodes depict the questions asked and the edges represent the decisions (yes/no). Leaf nodes determine the final class of the unknown entry. Following is a classic textbook example of a decision tree:

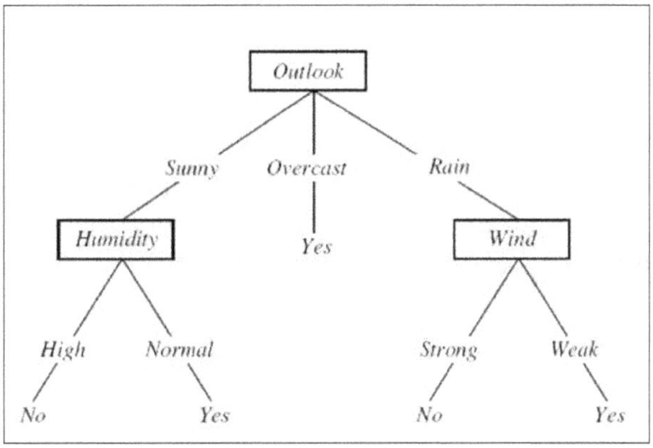

The preceding figure depicts the decision whether we can play lawn tennis or not, based on several attributes such as **Outlook**, **Humidity**, and **Wind**. Now the question that you may have is why outlook was chosen as the root node of the tree. The reason was that by choosing outlook as the first feature/attribute to split the dataset, the outcomes were split more evenly than if the split had been done with other attributes such as "humidity" or "wind".

The process of finding the attribute that can split the dataset more evenly than others is guided by entropy. Lesser the entropy, better the parameter. Entropy is known as the measure of information gain. It is calculated by the following formula:

$$H(X) = \sum_i P(x_i) I(x_i) = -\sum_i P(x_i) \log_b P(x_i)$$

Here $P(x_i)$ stands for the probability of x_i and $I(x_i)$ denotes the information gain.

Let's take the example of tennis dataset from Weka. Following is the file in the CSV format:

```
outlook,temperature,humidity,wind,playTennis
sunny, hot, high, weak, no
sunny, hot, high, strong, no
overcast, hot, high, weak, yes
rain, mild, high, weak, yes
```

```
rain,cool, normal, weak, yes
rain, cool, normal, strong, no
overcast, cool, normal, strong, yes
sunny, mild, high, weak, no
sunny, cool, normal, weak, yes
rain, mild, normal, weak, yes
sunny, mild, normal, strong, yes
overcast, mild, high, strong, yes
overcast, hot, normal, weak, yes
rain, mild, high, strong, no
```

You can see from the dataset that out of 14 instances (there are 14 rows in the file), 5 instances had the value `no` for `playTennis` and 9 instances had the value `yes`. Thus, the overall information is given by the following formula:

$$-\left(\frac{9}{14}\log_2\frac{9}{14}+\frac{5}{14}\log_2\frac{5}{14}\right)$$

This roughly evaluates to 0.94. Now from the next steps, we must pick the attribute that maximizes the information gain. Information gain is denoted as the difference between the total entropy and the entropy calculated for each possible split.

Let's go with one example. For the outlook attribute, there are three possible values: `rain`, `sunny`, and `overcast`, and for each of these values, the value of the attribute `playTennis` is either `no` or `yes`.

For `rain`, out of `5` instances, `3` instances have the value `yes` for the attribute `playTennis`; thus, the entropy is as follows:

$$-\left(\frac{3}{5}\log_2\frac{3}{5}+\frac{2}{5}\log_2\frac{2}{5}\right)$$

This is equal to 0.97.

For `overcast`, every instance has the value `yes`:

$$-\left(\frac{4}{4}\log_2\frac{4}{4}\right)$$

This is equal to 0.0.

For `sunny`, out of `5` instances, only `2` have the value `yes`:

$$-\left(\frac{2}{5}\log_2\frac{2}{5}+\frac{3}{5}\log_2\frac{3}{5}\right)$$

So the expected new entropy is given by the following formula:

$$\frac{4}{14}\times 0.0+\frac{5}{14}\times 0.97+\frac{5}{14}\times 0.97$$

This is roughly equal to 0.69. If you follow these steps for the other attributes, you will find that the new entropies are like as follows:

Attribute	**Entropy**	**Information gain**
outlook	0.69	0.94 - 0.69 => 0.25
temperature	0.91	0.94 - 0.91 => 0.03
humidity	0.724	0.94 - 0.725 => 0.215
windy	0.87	0.94 - 0.87 => 0.07

So the highest information gain is attained if we split the dataset based on the outlook attribute.

Sometimes multiple trees are constructed by generating a random subset of all the available features. This technique is known as random forest.

Linear regression

Regression is used to predict the target value of the real valued variable. For example, let's say we have data about the number of bedrooms and the total area of many houses in a locality. We also have their prices listed as follows:

Number of Bedrooms	**Total Area in square feet**	**Price**
2	1150	2300000
3	2500	5600000
3	1780	4571030
4	3000	9000000

Now let's say we have this data in a real estate site's database and we want to create a feature to predict the price of a new house with three bedrooms and total area of 1650 square feet.

Linear regression is used to solve these types of problems. As you can see, these types of problems are pretty common.

In linear regression, you start with a model where you represent the target variable—the variable for which you want to predict the value. A polynomial model is selected that minimizes the least square error (this will be explained later in the chapter). Let me walk you through this example.

Each row of the available data can be represented as a tuple where the first few elements represent the value of the known/input parameters and the last parameter shows the value of the price (the target variable). So taking inspiration from mathematics, we can represent the unknown with x and known as y. Thus, each row can be represented as $x_1, x_2, x_3, \ldots, x_n \mid y$ where x_1 to x_n represent the parameters (the total area and the number of bedrooms) and y represents the target value (the price of the house). Linear regression works on a model where y is represented with the x values.

The hypothesis is represented by an equation as the following. Here x_1 and theta denotes the input parameters (the number of bedrooms and the total area in square feet) and $h(x)$ represents the predicted value of the new house.

$$h(x) = \theta_0 + \theta_1 \times x_1 + \theta_2 \times x_2$$

Note that this hypothesis is still a polynomial model and we are just using two features: the number of bedrooms and the total area represented by x_1 and x_2.

So the square error is calculated by the following formula:

$$\sum \left(h(x) - y \right)^2$$

The task of linear regression is to choose a set of values for the coefficients θ which minimizes this error. The algorithm that minimizes this error is called gradient descent or batch gradient descent. You will learn more about it in *Chapter 2, Linear Regression.*

Logistic regression

Unlike linear regression, logistic regression predicts a Boolean value indicating the class/tag/category of the target variable. Logistic regression is one of the most popular binary classifiers and is modelled by the equation that follows. x_i and y_i stands for the independent input variables and their classes/tags respectively. Logistic regression is discussed at length in *Chapter 3, Classification Techniques.*

$$\prod_{i=1}^{n}\left[\frac{1}{1+e^{-x_i}\theta}\right]^{y_i}\times\left[1-\frac{1}{1+e^{-x_i}\theta}\right]^{1-y_i}$$

Recommender systems

Whenever you buy something from the web (say Amazon), it recommends you stuff that you might find interesting and might eventually buy as well. This is the result of recommender system. Let's take the following example of a movie rating:

Movie	Bob	Lucy	Jane	Jennifer	Jacob
Paper Towns	1	3	4	2	1
Focus	2	5	?	3	2
Cinderella	2	?	4	2	3
Jurrasic World	3	1	4	5	?
Die Hard	5	?	4	5	5

So in this toy example, we have 5 users and they have rated 5 movies. But not all the users have rated all the movies. For example, Jane hasn't rated "Focus" and Jacob hasn't rated "Jurassic World". The task of a recommender system is to initially guess what would be the ratings for the movies that aren't rated by the user and then recommend movies that have a guessed rating which is beyond a threshold (say 3).

There are several algorithms to solve this problem. One popular algorithm is known as **collaborative filtering** where the algorithm takes clues from the other user ratings. You will learn more about this in *Chapter 5, Collaborative Filtering*.

Unsupervised learning

As the name suggests, unlike supervised learning, unsupervised learning works on data that is not labeled or that doesn't have a category associated with each training example.

Unsupervised learning is used to understand data segmentation based on a few features of the data. For example, a supermarket might want to understand how many different types of customers they have. For that, they can use the following two features:

- The number of visits per month (number of times the customer shows up)
- The average bill amount

The initial data that the supermarket had might look like the following in a spreadsheet:

Visits	Average Bill
34	34.13
2	3400
3	2500
79	4.24
5	1200

So the data plotted in these 2 dimensions, after being clustered, might look like this following image:

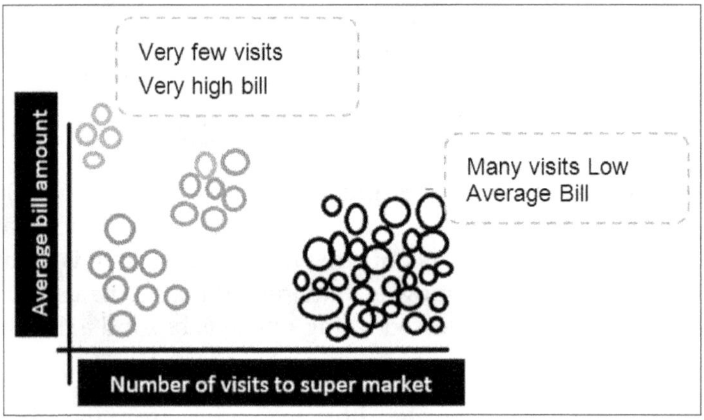

Here you see that there are 4 types of people with two extreme cases that have been annotated in the preceding image. Those who are very thorough and disciplinarian and know what they want, go to the store very few times and buy what they want, and generally their bills are very high. The vast majority falls under the basket where people make many trips (kind of like darting into a super market for a packet of chips, maybe) but their bills are really low. This type of information is crucial for the super market because they can optimize their operations based on these data.

This type of segmenting task has a special name in machine learning. It is called "clustering". There are several clustering algorithms and **K Means Clustering** is quite popular. The only flip side of k Means Clustering is that the number of possible clusters has to be told in the beginning.

Machine learning frameworks

I will be using the following machine learning frameworks to solve some of the real problems throughout the book:

- Accord.NET (`http://accord-framework.net/`)
- WekaSharp (`http://accord-framework.net/`)

You are much better off using these frameworks than creating your own because a lot of work has been done and they are used in the industry. So if you pick up using these frameworks along the way while learning about machine learning algorithms in general, that's a great thing. You will be in luck.

Machine learning for fun and profit

Machine learning requires a lot of data and most of the time you, as the developer of an algorithm, will not have the time to synthesize or obtain good data. However, you are in luck. Kaggle does that for you. Kaggle is a website where companies host several machine learning problems and they provide training and test data to test your algorithm. Some competitions are linked with employment. So if your model stands out, you stand a chance to interview with the company that hosted the competition. Here is a short list of companies that are using kaggle for their data science/machine learning problems:

A few of our clients | GE | MasterCard | Allstate | MERCK | amazon | facebook | Microsoft | Neiman Marcus

The next section gets you started with a kaggle competition; getting the data and solving it.

Recognizing handwritten digits – your "Hello World" ML program

Handwritten digits can be recognized with k-nearest neighbor algorithm.

Each handwritten digit is written on a 28*28 matrix. So there are 28*28 -> 784 pixels and each of these are represented as a single column of the dataset. Thus, the dataset has 785 columns. The first column is the label/digit and the remaining 784 values are the pixel values.

Following is a small example. Let's say, if we're to imagine this example as an 8 by 8 matrix, we would have something like the following figure for the digit 2:

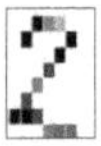

A matrix can be represented as a 2-D array where each pixel is represented by each cell. However, any 2-D array can be visually unwrapped to be a 1-D array where the length of the array is the product of the length and the breadth of the array. For example, for the 8 by 8 matrix, the size of the single dimensional array will be 64. Now if we store several images and their 2D matrix representations, we will have something as shown in the following spreadsheet:

	A	B	C	D	E	F	G
1	Label	Pixel1	Pixel2	Pixel3	Pixel4	...	Pixel64
2	2	85.92679	0	0	16.50806	97.16278	31.14512
3	3	47.47406	50.22488	0	0	77.28356	14.00682
4							

The header **Label** denotes the number and the remaining values are the pixel values. Lesser the pixel values, the darker the cell is in the pictorial representation of the number 2, as shown previously.

In this program, you will write code to solve the digit recognizer challenge from Kaggle, available at:

`https://www.kaggle.com/c/digit-recognizer.`

Once you get there, download the data and save it in some folder. We will be using the `train.csv` file (You can get the file from `www.kaggle.com/c/digit-recognizer/data`) for training our classifier. In this example, you will implement the k nearest neighbor algorithm from scratch, and then deploy this algorithm to recognize the digit.

For your convenience, I have pasted the code at `https://gist.github.com/sudipto80/72e6e56d07110baf4d4d`.

Following are the steps to create the classifier:

1. Open Visual Studio 2013.
2. Create a new project:

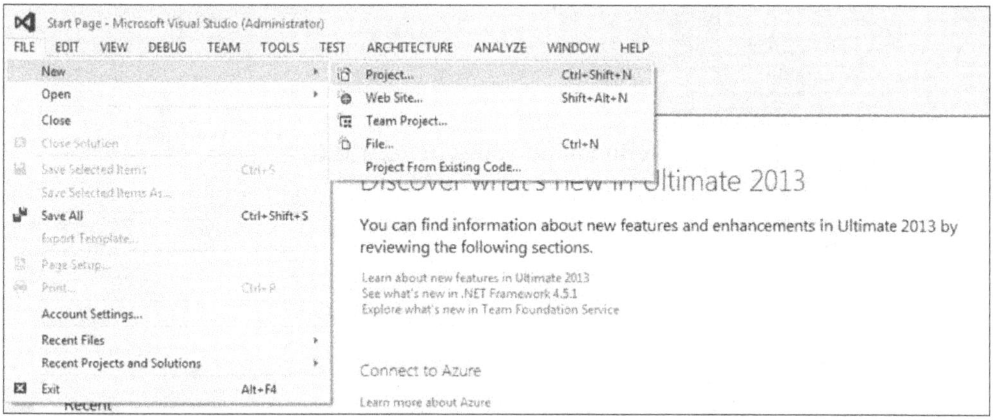

3. Select F# and give a name for the console app:

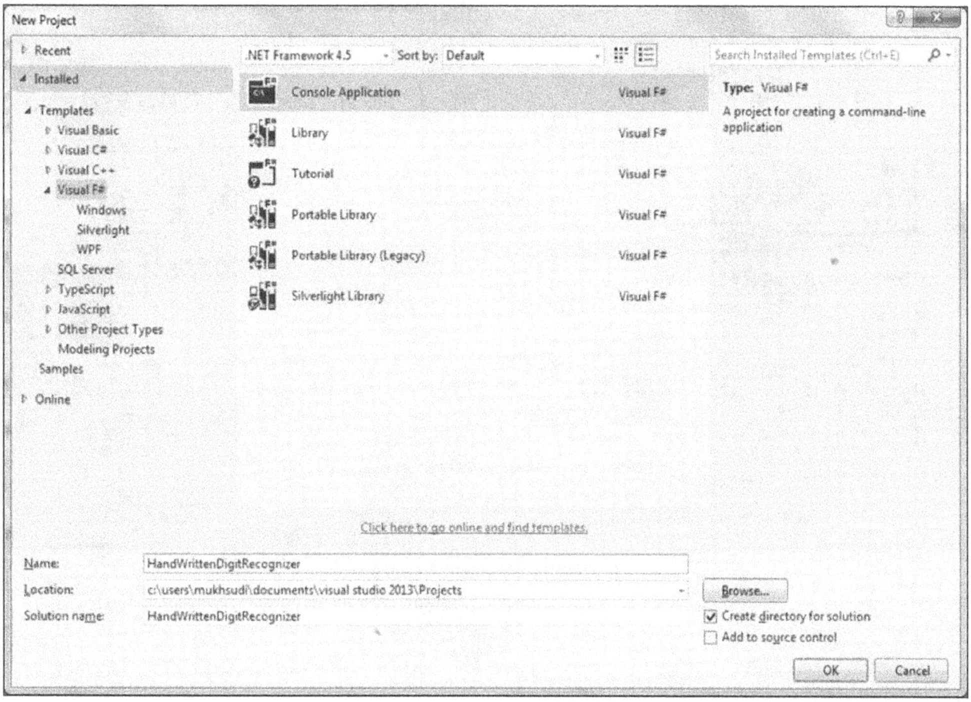

4. Once you create the project by clicking "**OK**", your `program.fs` file will look as the following image:

```
Program.fs
// Learn more about F# at http://fsharp.net
// See the 'F# Tutorial' project for more help.

[<EntryPoint>]
let main argv =
    printfn "%A" argv
    0 // return an integer exit code
```

5. Add the following functions and types in your file:

```
open System.IO
open System
open System.Windows.Forms
open System.Drawing

//The type that represents each row of the training
//or the test dataset
type Entry = {Label :string; Values : int list}

//Calculates Squared Euclidean distance between pixel
//values of two images
let distance ( values1 : int list  , values2 : int list) =
    values1
    |> List.zip values2
    |> List.map ( fun it -> Math.Pow( float (fst it) - float (snd it),2.0))
    |> List.sum
```

```
//Loading values from the training/test data.
//This assumes that the first one is the
//label/class/category of the data
let loadValues (filename : string) =
           File.ReadAllLines(filename)
                |> Seq.ofArray
                // leave the first row as that's the column headers
                |> Seq.skip (1)
                |> Seq.map ( fun line ->
                    {
                       Label =  line.Substring(0,line.IndexOf(','));
                       Values = line.Split(',')
                                 |> Seq.ofArray
                                 //the first token is the label. So skip it
                                 |> Seq.skip (1)
                                 |> Seq.map( fun n -> Convert.ToInt32(n))
                                 |> Seq.toList
                    })
                |>Seq.toList
```

```
//A generic k-nearest neighbor algorithm
let kNN ( entries : Entry list, newEntry : string * int[] , k : int) =
    entries  |> List.map( fun x -> ( x.Label, distance  (x.Values, snd (newEntry)
                                                                  |>Array.toList )))
             |> List.sortBy ( fun x -> snd x)
             |> Seq.ofList
             |> Seq.take k
             |> Seq.countBy (fun x -> fst x)
             |> Seq.toList
```

```
//Draws the digit
let drawDigit (pixels:float[], label:string) =
        let tile = 20
        let form = new Form(TopMost = true,
                            Visible = true,
                            Width = 29 * tile,
                            Height = 29 * tile)

        let panel = new Panel(Dock = DockStyle.Fill)
        panel.BackColor <- Color.Black
        form.Controls.Add(panel)
        let graphics = panel.CreateGraphics()
        pixels
        |> Array.iteri (fun i p ->
            let col = i % 28
            let row = i / 28
            let color = Color.FromArgb(int p, int p, int p)
            let brush = new SolidBrush(color)
            graphics.FillRectangle(brush,col*tile,row*tile,tile,tile))
        let point = new PointF((float32)5, (float32)5)
        let font = new Font(family = FontFamily.GenericSansSerif, emSize = (float32)30)
        graphics.DrawString(label, font, new SolidBrush(Color.YellowGreen), point)
        form.Show()
```

6. Finally, in the `main` method, add the following code:

```
//Point to the "train.csv" on your disk
let loaded =  loadValues @"C:\personal\train.csv"
//Here is the unknown entry and its pixel values for
//all 28 by 28 values.
//This entry depicts a "9" from the training dataset.

let newEntry = ("X",[|0;0;0;0;0;0;0;0;0;0;0;0;0;0;0;0;0;0;0;

let pixels = snd(newEntry) |> Array.map (fun t -> float t)
//Let's consider only 5 nearest neighbors
let k = 5
//Getting back the labels for each of the nearest neighbours
let labels = kNN (loaded , newEntry, k)
//Locating the guess. The one with the maximum votes
let guess = fst(  labels |> List.item 0)
//Answer will be 9
drawDigit (pixels , "I think that it is a " + guess)
Console.ReadLine() |> ignore
```

When this program runs, it will produce the following output:

How does this work?

The `distance` function is based on the Euclidean distance function, as mentioned earlier in the chapter. Now you see that a general purpose Euclidean distance function is coded in the distance function. You might have noticed that there is a small difference between the formula and the implementation. The implementation finds the squared Euclidean distance given by the following formula:

$$d^2(p,q) = (p_1 - q_1)^2 + (p_2 - q_2)^2 + \cdots + (p_i - q_i)^2 + \cdots + (p_n - q_n)^2$$

Here p and q denote the two vectors. In this case, p might denote one example from the training set and q might denote the test example or the new uncategorized data that we have depicted by `newEntry` in the preceding code.

The `loadValues` function loads the pixel values and the category for each training/test data, and creates a list of `Entry` types from the CSV file.

The k-NN algorithm is implemented in the `kNN` function. Refer to the following line of code:

```
|> List.map( fun x -> ( x.Label, distance  (x.Values, snd
(newEntry) |>Array.toList )))
```

This preceding code creates a list of tuples where the first element is the category of the entry and the second is the distance square value for the test data from each of the training entry. So it might look as follows:

1	Label	Distance from Test Data
2	9	0.34
3	9	0.23
4	4	4.55
5	4	22.21
6	4	11.13
7	9	2.10
8	9	1.69

Now consider the following line:

```
|> List.sortBy ( fun x -> snd x)
```

It sorts this list of tuples based on the increasing distance from the test data. Thus, the preceding list will become as shown in the following image:

1	Label	Distance from Test Data
2	9	0.23
3	9	0.34
4	9	1.69
5	9	2.10
6	4	4.55
7	4	11.13
8	4	22.21

If you see, there are four 9s and three 4s in this list. The following line transforms this list into a histogram:

```
|> Seq.countBy (fun x -> fst x)
```

So if k is chosen to be 5, then we will have four 9s and one 4. Thus, k nearest neighbor will conclude that the digit is probably a "9" since most of the nearest neighbors are "9".

The `drawDigit` function draws the digit pixel by pixel and writes out the guessed label for the digit. It does so by drawing each pixel on a tile size of 20.

Summary

In this chapter, you have learnt about several different types of machine learning techniques and their possible usages. Try to spot probable machine learning algorithms that might be deployed deep inside some applications. Following are some examples of machine learning. Your mailbox is curated by an automatic spam protector and it learns every time you move an e-mail from your inbox to the spam folder. This is an example of a supervised classification algorithm. When you apply for a health insurance, then based on several parameters, they (the insurance company) try to fit your data and predict what premium you might have to pay. This is an example of linear regression. Sometimes when people buy baby diapers at supermarkets, they get a discount coupon for buying beer. Sounds crazy, right! But the machine learning algorithm figured out that people who buy the diapers buy beer too. So they want to provoke the users to buy more. There is lot of buzz right now about predictive analytics. It is nothing but predicting an event in the future by associating a probability score. For example, figuring out how long will a shopper take to return to the store for her next purchase. These data are extracted from the visit patterns. That's unsupervised learning working in the background.

Sometimes one simple algorithm doesn't provide the needed accuracy. So then several methods are used and a special class of algorithm, known as Ensemble method, is used to club the individual results. In loose terms, it kind of resonates with the phrase "crowd-smart". You will learn about some ensemble methods in a later chapter.

I want to wrap up this chapter with the following tip. When you have a problem that you want to solve and you think machine learning can help, follow the following steps. Break the problem into smaller chunks and then try to locate a class of machine learning problem domain for this smaller problem. Then find the best method in that class to solve. Iterate over and over until your error rates are within permissible limits. And then wrap it in a nice application/user interface.

2
Linear Regression

"Honey! How much will gasoline cost next year?"

Linear regression is a technique to predict the value of a feature/attribute in a continuous range. It is similar to classification in a way that both types of algorithms solve a similar problem. But classification yields a discrete value as the tag while regression tries to predict a real value. In this chapter, you will learn how linear regression works and how it can be used in real-life settings.

Objective

After reading this chapter, you will be able to understand how several linear regression algorithms work and how to tune your linear regression model. You will also learn to use some parts of **Math.NET** and **Accord.NET**, which make implementing some of the linear regression algorithms simple. Along the way, you will also learn how to use FsPlot to plot various charts. All source code is made available at `https://gist.github.com/sudipto80/3b99f6bbe9b21b76386d`.

Different types of linear regression algorithms

Based on the approach used and the number of input parameters, there are several types of linear regression algorithms to determine the real value of the target variable. In this chapter, you will learn how to implement the following algorithms using F#:

- Simple Least Square Linear Regression
- Multiple Linear Regression

- Weighted Linear regression
- Ridge Regression
- Multivariate Multiple Linear Regression

These algorithms will be implemented using a robust industry standard open source .NET mathematics API called Math.NET. Math.NET has an F# friendly wrapper.

APIs used

In this chapter, you will learn how to use the preceding APIs to solve problems using several linear regression methods and plot the result.

FsPlot JavaScript charting library for F#

FsPlot is a charting library for F# to generate charts using industry standard JavaScript charting APIs, such as HighCharts. FsPlot provides a nice interface to generate several combination charts, which is very useful when trying to understand the linear regression model. You can find more details about the API at its homepage at `https://github.com/TahaHachana/FsPlot`.

Math.NET Numerics for F# 3.7.0

Math.NET Numerics is the numerical foundation of the Math.NET project, aiming to provide methods and algorithms for numerical computations in science, in engineering, and in everyday use. It supports F# 3.0 on .Net 4.0, .Net 3.5, and Mono on Windows, Linux, and Mac; Silverlight 5 and Windows 8 with PCL portable profile 47; Android/iOS with Xamarin.

You can get the API from the NuGet page at `https://www.nuget.org/packages/MathNet.Numerics.FSharp/`. For more details, visit the project homepage at `http://www.mathdotnet.com/`.

The **Accord.NET** framework is a .NET machine learning framework combined with audio and image processing libraries completely written in C#. It is a complete framework for building production-grade computer vision, computer audition, signal processing, and statistics applications; it is for commercial use as well. For more details, visit the homepage of the framework at `http://accord-framework.net/`.

Getting Math.NET

Math.NET is a leading .NET API for doing mathematical, statistical, and of course machine learning stuff. Math.NET, like any other .NET API, can be used in C# and F#. But there is a nice wrapper for F# that makes the experience in F# very friendly. You can get that F# wrapper (called `Math.Net.Numerics.FSharp`) from NuGet at `https://www.nuget.org/packages/MathNet.Numerics.FSharp/`.

Experimenting with Math.NET

In the following section, you will learn how to do several basic matrix-related and vector-related operations using Math.NET.

The basics of matrices and vectors (a short and sweet refresher)

Using Math.Net numerics, you can create matrices and vectors easily. The following section shows how. However, before you can create the vector or the matrix using Math.NET API, you have to reference the library properly. The examples in this chapter run using the F# script.

You have to write the following code at the beginning of the file and then run these in the F# interactive:

```
#load "...\packages\MathNet.Numerics.FSharp.3.10.0\MathNet.Numerics.fsx"
open MathNet.Numerics.LinearAlgebra
```

Creating a vector

You can create a vector as follows:

```
let velocities = vector[23.;4.;5.;2.]
```

The vector values must always be `float` as per Math.NET. Once you run this in the F# interactive, it will create the following output:

```
val velocities : Vector<float> = DenseVector 4-Double
23
 4
 5
 2
```

Creating a matrix

A matrix can be created in several ways using the Math.NET package. In the examples in this chapter, you will see the following ways most often:

- **Creating a matrix by hand**: A matrix can be created manually using the Math.Net F# package, as follows:

```
let y = matrix [[1.;3.]
                [1.;5.]
                [1.;4.]]
```

  Once you run this, you will get the following in the F# interactive:

```
val y : Matrix<float> = DenseMatrix 3x2-Double
1  3
1  5
1  4
```

- **Creating a matrix from a list of rows**: A matrix can also be created from a given list of rows. Normally, matrices that are generally expected to be filled with mostly non-zero values are known as `DenseMatrix`.

  Here is how to create a dense matrix from an array or rows.

  The following is the mileage data of several cars. This data is available at `https://archive.ics.uci.edu/ml/machine-learning-databases/auto-mpg/auto-mpg.data`.

```
18.0   8   307.0      130.0      3504.      12.0   70  1    "chevrolet chevelle malibu"
15.0   8   350.0      165.0      3693.      11.5   70  1    "buick skylark 320"
18.0   8   318.0      150.0      3436.      11.0   70  1    "plymouth satellite"
16.0   8   304.0      150.0      3433.      12.0   70  1    "amc rebel sst"
17.0   8   302.0      140.0      3449.      10.5   70  1    "ford torino"
15.0   8   429.0      198.0      4341.      10.0   70  1    "ford galaxie 500"
14.0   8   454.0      220.0      4354.       9.0   70  1    "chevrolet impala"
```

  The following are the column descriptions:

```
1. mpg:           continuous
2. cylinders:     multi-valued discrete
3. displacement:  continuous
4. horsepower:    continuous
5. weight:        continuous
6. acceleration:  continuous
7. model year:    multi-valued discrete
8. origin:        multi-valued discrete
9. car name:      string (unique for each instance)
```

  You can get these details at `https://archive.ics.uci.edu/ml/machine-learning-databases/auto-mpg/auto-mpg.names`.

  As you can see, apart from the name column, everything is real valued and thus can be loaded in a `DenseMatrix`. So if we get rid of the last column and remove the rows with missing values, then we can load the entire matrix using the command that follows.

I have modified the file by deleting all the rows with missing values (missing values are denoted by ?) and then delimiting the file with commas instead of multiple white spaces. You can download the file with the book's source code.

```
//Loading values of the csv file and generating a dense matrix
//Please modify the file path to point it in your local disc
let rows = File.ReadAllLines("C:\\mpg.csv")
                |> Array.map ( fun t -> t.Split(',')
```

```
                                          |> Array.map(fun t -> float t))

let mpgData = DenseMatrix.ofRowArrays rows
```

Finding the transpose of a matrix

Finding the transpose of a matrix is very important because we have to rely on this function a lot while implementing several linear regression algorithms. A transpose is nothing but rotating of the matrix. So in a transposed matrix, the rows of the original matrix become the columns, and the columns of the original matrix become the rows.

$$\begin{bmatrix} 1 & 2 & 3 \\ 4 & 5 & 6 \\ 7 & 8 & 9 \end{bmatrix}$$

Transposing will produce this:

$$\begin{bmatrix} 1 & 4 & 7 \\ 2 & 5 & 8 \\ 3 & 6 & 9 \end{bmatrix}$$

Using Math.NET, you can declare the first matrix and then calculate the transpose of the matrix as follows:

```
let myMat = matrix [[1. ;2.; 3.]
                    [4. ;5.; 6.]
                    [7. ;8.; 9.]]

let myMat' = myMat.Transpose()
```

Finding the inverse of a matrix

Only square matrices can be inversed. And if the determinant of the matrix is zero then the elements of the inversed matrix can be infinity or negative infinity or NaN (Not a Number).

Here is an example of finding the inverse using Math.NET:

```
let myMat = matrix [[1.;2.;3.]
                    [4.;5.;2.]
                    [7.;0.8;9.]]

let myMat' = myMat.Inverse()
```

When run in the F# interactive, this snippet will produce the following result:

```
val myMat : Matrix<float> =
  DenseMatrix 3x3-Double
1    2  3
4    5  2
7  0.8  9

val myMat' : Matrix<float> =
  DenseMatrix 3x3-Double
-0.452083    0.1625   0.114583
 0.229167     0.125  -0.104167
  0.33125   -0.1375    0.03125
```

Trace of a matrix

The trace of a matrix is the sum of the diagonal elements. The trace can be calculated with the function `Trace()` as follows:

```
let myMat = matrix [[1. ;2.; 3.]
                    [4. ;5.; 2.]
                    [7. ;0.8; 9.]]

let myMatTrace = myMat.Trace()
```

QR decomposition of a matrix

The general linear regression model calculation requires us to find the inverse of the matrix, which can be computationally expensive for bigger matrices. A decomposition scheme, such as QR and SVD, helps in that regard.

QR decomposition breaks a given matrix into two different matrices—Q and R, such that when these two are multiplied, the original matrix is found.

$$X = Q\begin{bmatrix} R \\ 0 \end{bmatrix}$$

In the preceding image, *X* is an n x p matrix with n rows and p columns, *R* is an upper diagonal matrix, and *Q* is an n x n matrix given by:

$$\begin{bmatrix} Q1 & Q2 \end{bmatrix}$$

Here, Q1 is the first p columns of Q and Q2 is the last n - p columns of Q.

Using the Math.Net method QR you can find QR factorization:

```
let myMat = matrix  [[1.0;2.0;3.0]
                      [4.0;5.0;2.0]
                      [7.0;0.8;9.0]]

let qr = myMat.QR()
```

Just to prove the fact that you will get the original matrix back, you can multiply Q and R to see if you get the original matrix back:

```
let myMatAgain = qr.Q * qr.R
```

SVD of a matrix

SVD stands for Single Value Decomposition. In this a matrix, X is represented by three matrices (the definition of SVD is taken from Wikipedia).

Suppose M is an m × n matrix whose entries come from the field K, which is either the field of real numbers or the field of complex numbers. Then there exists a factorization, called a singular value decomposition of M, of the following form:

$$M = U\Sigma V^*$$

In this preceding formula, you will find the following:

- **U** is an m × m unitary matrix.
- **Σ** is an m × n diagonal matrix with non-negative real numbers on the diagonal.
- **V*** is an n × n unitary matrix over K (If K = R, unitary matrices are orthogonal matrices). V* is the conjugate transpose of the n × n unitary matrix, V.

The diagonal entries, σi, of Σ are known as the singular values of M. A common convention is to list singular values in descending order. In this case, the diagonal matrix, Σ, is uniquely determined by M (though not the matrices U and V).

$$X = U \begin{bmatrix} W \\ 0 \end{bmatrix} V'$$

Using Math.NET, you can find the decomposed values of SVD as shown next:

```
let myMat = matrix  [[1.0;2.0;3.0]
                     [4.0;5.0;2.0]
                     [7.0;0.8;9.0]]

let qr = myMat.QR()

let svdR = myMat.Svd(true)
//Gets the singular values of matrix in ascending value.
let s= svdR.S
//Gets the transpose right singular vectors
//(transpose of V, an n-by-n unitary matrix)
let v' = svdR.VT
//Gets the left singular vectors (U - m-by-m unitary matrix)
let u = svdR.U
//Returns the singular values as a diagonal Matrix<T>.
let w = svdR.W
//Generating the original matrix again
let myMatSVD = u*w*v'

printfn "%A" myMatSVD
```

SVD and QR decomposition of a matrix allow you to perform the multiple linear regression without performing the inverse of the matrix. Math.NET offers a couple of methods called **Svd** and **QR** to perform multiple linear regression using these decomposition schemes.

Linear regression method of least square

Let's say you have a list of data point pairs such as the following:

$$\{(x_1, y_1)(x_2, y_2)(x_3, y_3), ..., (x_n, y_n)\}$$

You want to find out if there are any linear relationships between x and y.

In the simplest possible model of linear regression, there exists a simple linear relationship between the independent variable x (also known as the predictor variable) and the dependent variable y (also known as the predicted or the target variable). The independent variable is most often represented by the symbol x and the target variable is represented by the symbol y. In the simplest form of linear regression, with only one predictor variable, the predicted value of *Y* is calculated by the following formula:

$$\hat{y} = b_0 + b_1 \times x$$

$\hat{y}$ is the predicted variable for y. Error for a single data point is represented by:

$$e_i = y_i - \hat{y}_i$$

b_0 and b_1 are the regression parameters that can be calculated with the following formula.

The best linear model minimizes the sum of squared errors. This is known as **Sum of Squared Error** (SSE).

$$\sum_{i=1}^{n} e_i^2 = \sum_{i=1}^{n} (y_i - b_0 - b_1 x_i)^2$$

For the best model, the regression coefficients are found by the following formula:

$$b_1 = \frac{\sum \overline{x}\,\overline{y} - n\overline{x}\,\overline{y}}{\sum x^2 - n\overline{x}^2}$$

$$b_0 = \overline{y} - b_1 x$$

Where each variable is described as the following:

$$\bar{x} = \frac{1}{n}\sum_{i=1}^{n} x_i \quad \bar{y} = \frac{1}{n}\sum_{i=1}^{n} y_i$$

$$\Sigma xy = \sum_{i=1}^{n} x_i y_i \quad \Sigma x^2 = \sum_{i=1}^{n} x_i^2$$

The best linear model reduces the residuals. A residual is the vertical gap between the predicted and the actual value. The following image shows very nicely what is meant by residual:

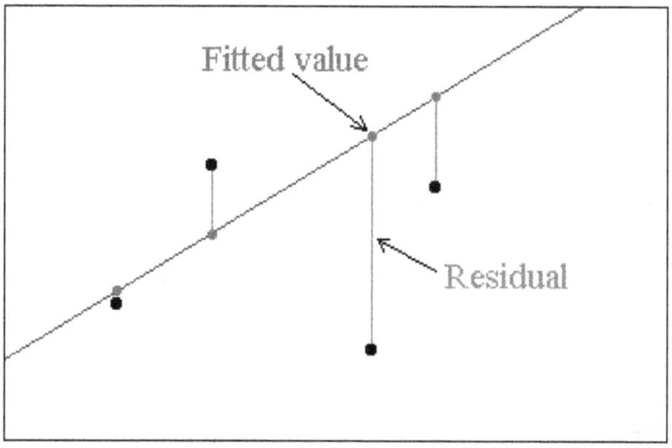

Finding linear regression coefficients using F#

The following is an example problem that can be solved using linear regression.

For seven programs, the amount of disk I/O operations and processor times were measured and the results were captured in a list of tuples. Here is that list: (14,2), (16,5),(27,7) (42,9), (39, 10), (50,13), (83,20). The task for linear regression is to fit a model for these data points.

For this experiment, you will write the solution using F# from scratch, building each block one at a time.

1. Create a new F# program script in LINQPad as shown and highlighted in the following image:

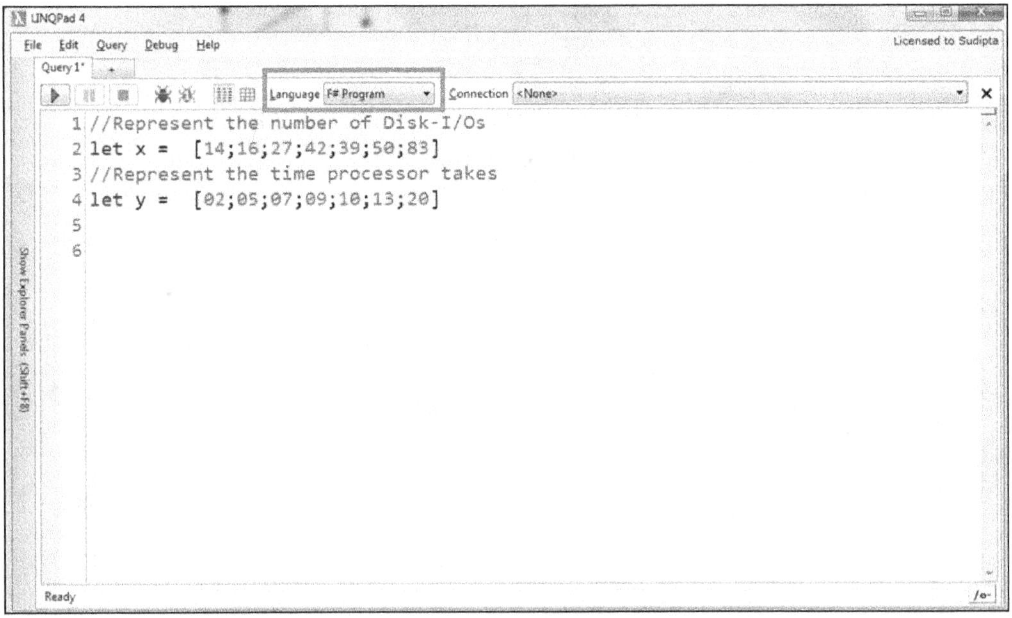

2. Add the following variables to represent the data points:

```
//Represent the number of Disk-I/Os
let x =  [14;16;27;42;39;50;83]
//Represent the time processor takes
let y =  [02;05;07;09;10;13;20]
```

3. Add the following code to find the values needed to calculate `b0` and `b1`:

```
let diff = List.zip x y
let xy = diff |> List.map ( fun it -> float (fst it) * float (snd it))
              |> List.sum
//Finds the average of the x values
let x_ = x |> List.map ( fun z -> float z)
           |> List.average
//Finds the average of the y values
let y_ = y |> List.map ( fun z -> float z)
           |> List.average
//Finds the sum of the squares of each values of x
let sx_2 = x |> List.sumBy ( fun  t -> float t * float t)
//Finds the sum of the squares of each values of y
let sy_2 = y |> List.sumBy ( fun t -> float t * float t)
//Finds the length of the vector
let n = float x.Length
//Calculates b1 as per the given formula
let b1 =  (xy - n*x_*y_)/(sx_2 - n * x_ * x_)
//Calculates b0 as per the given formula
let b0 = y_ - b1*x_
b1.Dump("b1")
b0.Dump("b0")
//Create a record type to project the result for each pair
type Entry = {
                DiskIO:int;
                CPUTime:int;
                //Estimate is the value obtained from recursion
                Estimate:float;
                //The absolute error. Can be negative
                Error : float;
                //Squared error.
                ErrorSquared:float
             }
//Calculate regression value for each of the pairs
//and project the result
let result = List.zip x y
              |> List.map (fun elem ->
                 {
                     DiskIO = fst elem;
                     CPUTime  = snd elem;
                     Estimate = b0 + b1 * float( fst elem);
                     Error = float(snd elem) - b0 - b1 * float (fst elem);
                     ErrorSquared = Math.Pow(float(snd elem) - b0 - b1 * float (fst elem),2.)
                 })

result.Dump("Result of the linear regression")
```

4. Once you do this, you will get the following output:

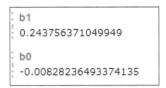

```
b1
0.243756371049949

b0
-0.00828236493374135
```

The following is the final output we receive:

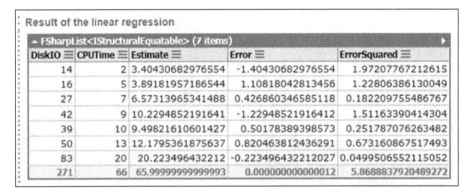

Result of the linear regression

FSharpList<IStructuralEquatable> (7 items)

DiskIO	CPUTime	Estimate	Error	ErrorSquared
14	2	3.40430682976554	-1.40430682976554	1.97207767212615
16	5	3.89181957186544	1.10818042813456	1.22806386130049
27	7	6.57313965341488	0.426860346585118	0.182209755486767
42	9	10.2294852191641	-1.22948521916412	1.51163390414304
39	10	9.49821610601427	0.50178389398573	0.251787076263482
50	13	12.1795361875637	0.820463812436291	0.673160867517493
83	20	20.223496432212	-0.223496432212027	0.0499506552115052
271	66	65.9999999999993	0.000000000000012	5.8688837920489272

Now in order to understand how good your linear regression model fits the data, we need to plot the actual data points as scatter plots and the regression line as a straight line.

I will be using **HighCharts** using FsPlot. FsPlot is a very nice wrapper that lets you draw HighCharts data. You can get FsPlot from NuGet.

1. Create a new F# **Tutorial** as seen in the following screenshot:

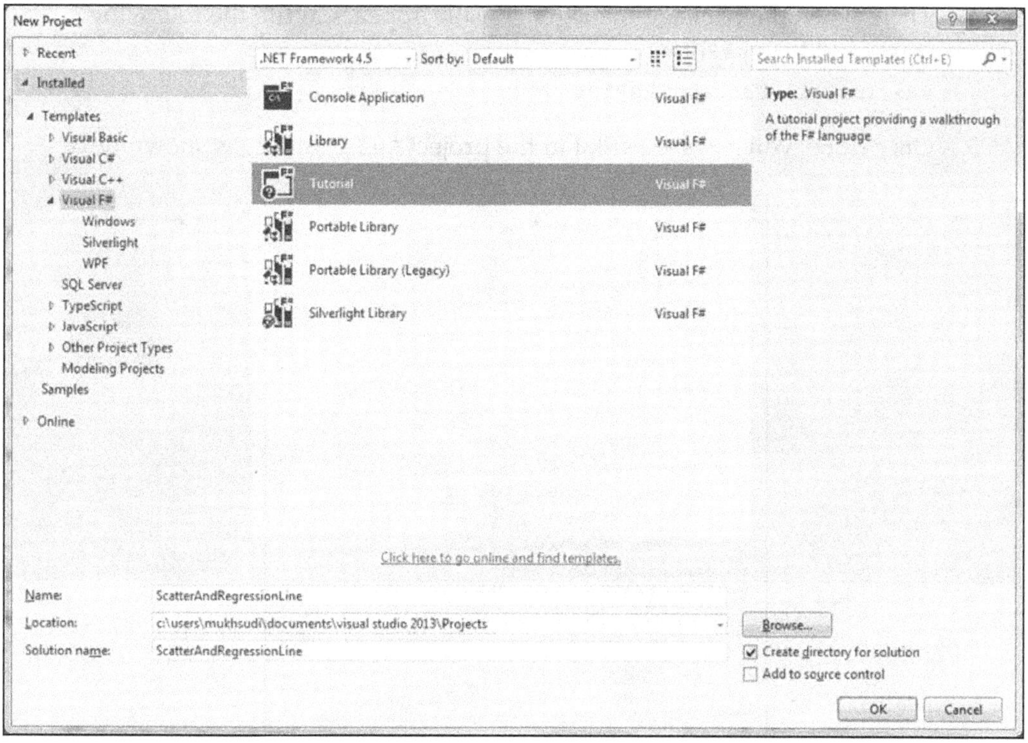

2. Once the project is created, add FsPlot from NuGet.
3. Go to **Tools** | **NuGet Package Manager** | **Package Manager Console**, as seen in the following screenshot:

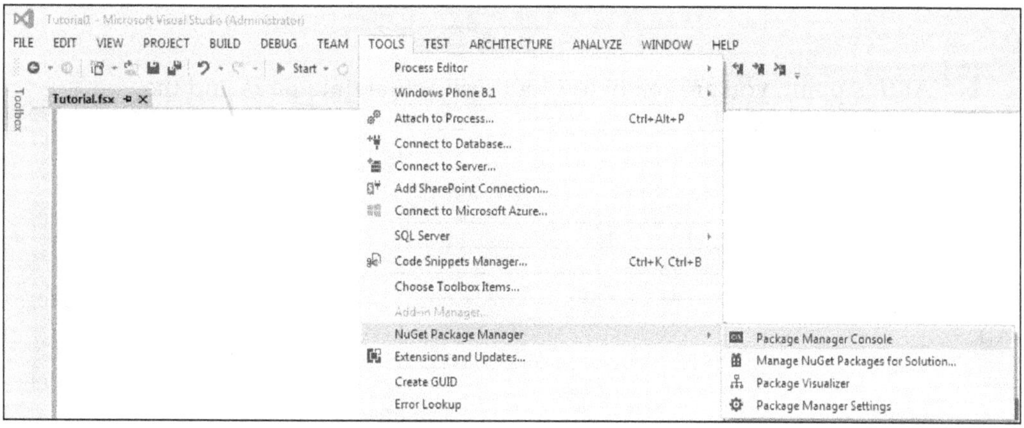

4. Then, when the package manager console appears, write the following command to get FsPlot:

```
PM> Install-Package FsPlot
```

5. Once done, you can see FsPlot in the project `References`, as shown next:

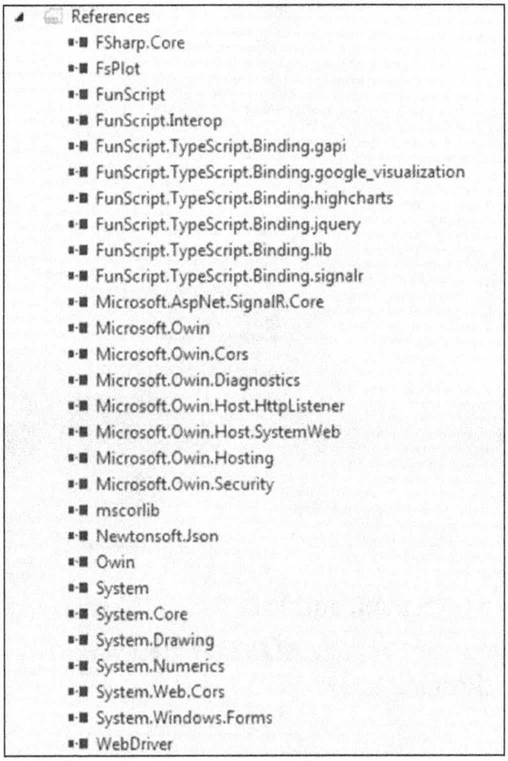

6. At this point, you are ready to plot those actual data pairs and the regression line:

```
open System
open FsPlot.Data
open FsPlot.Highcharts.Charting

let x =  [14;16;27;42;39;50;83]
let y =  [02;05;07;09;10;13;20]
let y' = [3;4;5;7;23;21;34]

//Here you shall be using the values of b0 and b1 calculated before
let b0 = -0.00828236493374135
let b1 = 0.243756371049949

let regressionPairs = x |> List.map ( fun xElem -> (xElem, b0 + b1* float xElem ))

let pairs = List.zip x y

let scatter = Series.Scatter pairs
let regressionLine = Series.Line regressionPairs

let chart =
    [scatter;regressionLine]
    |> Chart.Combine
    |> Chart.WithNames ["Actual data"; "Regression Line"]
    |> Chart.WithTitle "Processor Time and Disk I/O"
    |> Chart.WithLegend true
```

7. Select the entire code to run it in the F# interactive. Once done, it will generate the following chart:

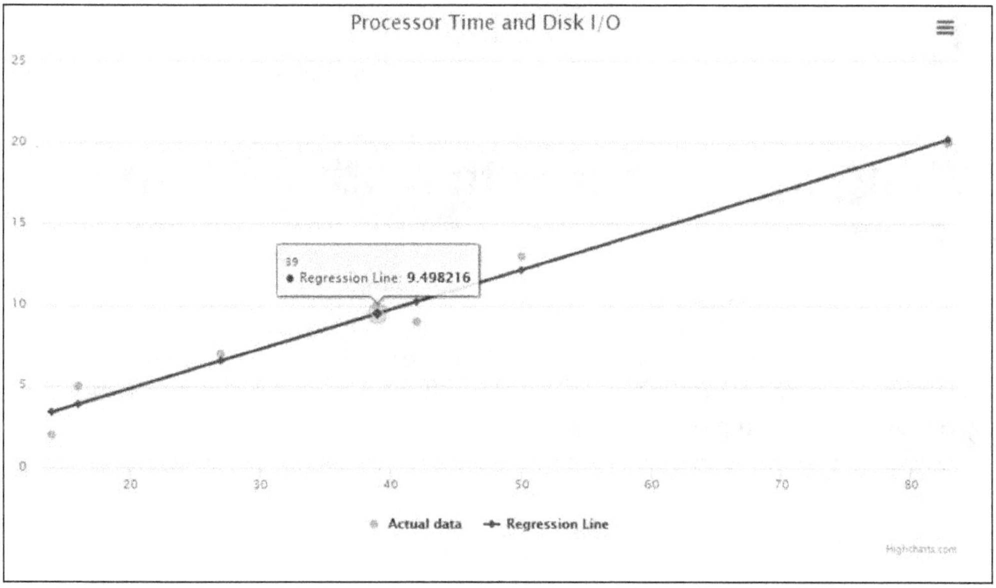

HighCharts animates the chart as it gets rendered. The chart is also interactive in nature, so you can hover your mouse on the line and the points will show up, as shown in the preceding screenshot. I have recorded the session and posted it at `http://recordit.co/SMNa4i7S8r` for you to see the chart being rendered in real time.

Finding the linear regression coefficients using Math.NET

In the previous example, we used F# to obtain `b0` and `b1` from the first principal. However, we can use Math.NET to find these values for us. The following code snippet does that for us in three lines of code:

```
let xV =  [|14.;16.;27.;42.;39.;50.;83.|]
let yV =  [|02.;05.;07.;09.;10.;13.;20.|]
let (b0,b1) = SimpleRegression.Fit(xV,yV)
```

This produces the following result in the F# interactive:

```
val xV : float [] = [|14.0; 16.0; 27.0; 42.0; 39.0; 50.0; 83.0|]
val yV : float [] = [|2.0; 5.0; 7.0; 9.0; 10.0; 13.0; 20.0|]
val b1 : float = 0.243756371
val b0 : float = -0.008282364934
```

Take a moment to note that the values are exactly the same as we calculated earlier.

Putting it together with Math.NET and FsPlot

In this example, you will see how Math.NET and FsPlot can be used together to generate the linear regression coefficients and plot the result. For this example, we will use a known relation between **Relative Humidity** (**RH**) and **Dew point temperature**. The relationship between relative humidity and dew point temperature is given by the following two formulas:

$$RH \approx 100 - 5(t - t_d)$$

Here, t and t_d are the temperatures in degrees Celsius.

t_d is dew point, which is a measure of atmospheric moisture. It is the temperature to which the air must be cooled in order to reach saturation (assuming the air pressure and the moisture content are constant).

Let's say the dew point is 10 degrees Celsius, then we can see how linear regression can be used to find a relationship between the temperature and RH.

The following code snippet generates a list of 50 random temperatures and then uses the formula to find the RH. It then feeds this data into a linear regression system to find the best fit for the data, and then finally plots all these data.

```
let genRandomTemps count =
    let rnd = System.Random()
    List.init count (fun _ -> rnd.Next (40,100))

let temps = genRandomTemps 50

let t_d = 19

let RH_Formula = temps |> List.map ( fun t -> float ((100 - 5 * ( t - t_d))))
                       |> List.toArray

let temp_Array = temps|>List.map ( fun t -> float t)
                      |>List.toArray

let from_Formula = Array.zip temp_Array RH_Formula

let (rhB0, rhB1) = SimpleRegression.Fit from_Formula

let regressionPairs = temp_Array |> Array.map ( fun t -> (t, rhB0 + rhB1* t ))

let formulaSpots  = Series.Scatter from_Formula
let regressionLine = Series.Line regressionPairs

let chart =
    [formulaSpots;regressionLine]
    |> Chart.Combine
    |> Chart.WithNames ["Actual data"; "Regression Line"]
    |> Chart.WithTitle "Predicting Relative Humidity"
    |> Chart.WithLegend true
```

This produces the following result:

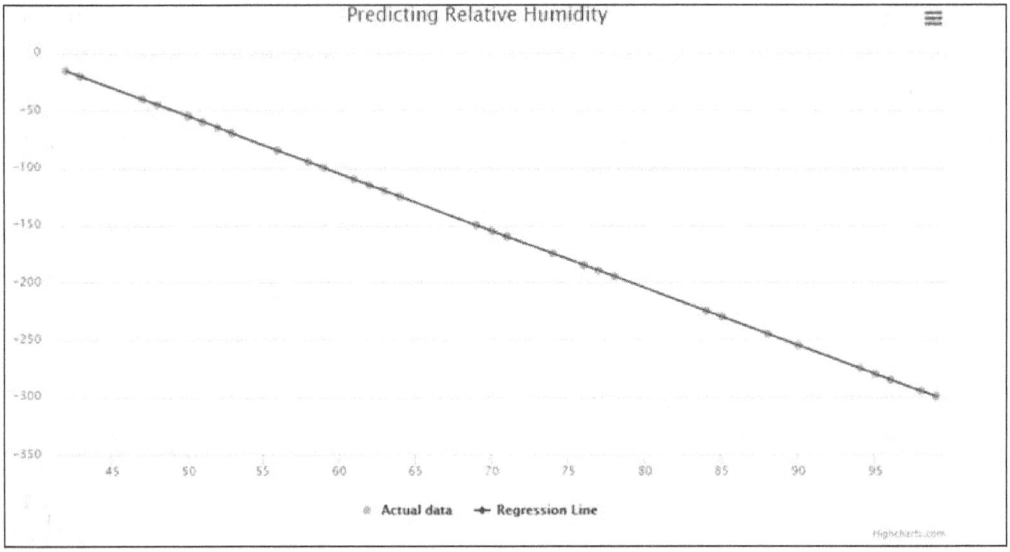

The values of `rhB0` and `rhB1` are as follows:

```
val rhB1 : float = -5.0
val rhB0 : float = 195.0
```

So the equation becomes 195.0 – 5*t, which is pretty close to the actual equation.

Multiple linear regression

Sometimes it makes more sense to include more predictors (that is, the independent variables) to find the value of the dependent variable (that is, the predicted variable). For example, predicting the price of a house based only on the total area is probably not a good idea. Maybe the price also depends on the number of bathrooms and the distance from several required facilities, such as schools, grocery stores, and so on.

So we might have a dataset as shown next, and the problem we pose for our linear regression model is to predict the price of a new house given all the other parameters:

Size	Bedrooms	Bathrooms	Distance_From_Scool	Distance_From_Grocery_Store	Price
2143	2	1	0.98344108	0.293775301	208
2410	2	2	0.304425464	0.076821232	208
1339	1	1	0.380983271	0.547134073	161
1822	5	2	0.271166043	0.396839619	190
1230	3	2	0.298155285	0.442560643	210
1733	2	2	0.268317226	0.959010297	72

In this case, the model can be represented as a linear combination of all the predictors, as follows:

$$y(x) = \theta_0 + \theta_1 x_1 + \theta_2 x_2 + \ldots + \theta_n x_n$$

Here, the theta values represent the parameters we must select to fit the model. In vectorized form, this can be written as:

$$Y = \theta' X$$

Theta can be calculated by the following formula:

$$\theta = (X'X)^{-1} X'Y$$

So using the `MathNet.Fsharp` package, this can be calculated as follows:

```
//Here we have the predictor variables
let X = matrix[[1. ;2.; 3.]
               [4. ;5.; 2.]
               [7. ;0.8; 9.]]
//This is the new set of predictor values for an observation
let X_unseen = vector [4.;5.;1.89]
//These are the values for the set of observations seen
let Y = matrix[[3.]
               [4.]
               [5.]]
//Calculating theta from the above formula
let theta  = ((X.Transpose() * X).Inverse() * X.Transpose()) * Y
//Calculating the prediction for the new Y for the new set of
//predictor values.
let predicted_Y = theta.Transpose() * X_unseen
```

Previously, in *Chapter 1, Introduction to Machine Learning,* I mentioned a car's miles per gallon (mpg) dataset. The question I want to solve with multiple linear regression is: what is the relationship between miles per gallon (mpg) and the following parameters:

- Cylinders: Multi-valued discrete
- Displacement: Continuous
- Horsepower: Continuous
- Weight: Continuous
- Acceleration: Continuous

The following program reads the first 350 rows of the dataset and tries to determine a model, and then uses this model to predict the miles per gallon for an unknown car:

```
let rows = File.ReadAllLines("C:\\mpgdata.csv")
                    |> Array.map ( fun t -> t.Split(',')|> Array.toSeq |> Seq.take 6
                                                |> Seq.toArray
                                                |> Array.map(fun t -> float t))
                    |> Array.toSeq
                    |> Seq.take 350
                    |> Seq.toArray
//A matrix is created with all the numeric columns and 350 rows
let created1 = DenseMatrix.ofRowArrays rows
//Values for the predicted variable is extracted.
let milesPerGallon = created1.Column(0)
//After extracting the predicted column let's remove it
//to get the matrix to calculate the theta
let created2 = created1.RemoveColumn(0)
//Storing predicted values in another variable
let Y_MPG = milesPerGallon
//Calculating Theta as per the given formula
let Theta_MPG = (created2.Transpose() * created2).Inverse()
                * created2.Transpose() * milesPerGallon
//Details on an unknown car
let unknownCarDetails = vector [4.;140.;90.;2264.;15.5]
//Calculating the predicted mpg value of the new unknown car
let predictedMPG = Theta_MPG * unknownCarDetails
```

Multiple linear regression and variations using Math.NET

As mentioned earlier, a regression model can be found using matrix decomposition such as QR and SVD.

The following code finds the theta from QR decomposition for the same data:

```
let qrlTheta = MultipleRegression.QR( created2 ,Y_MPG)
```

When run, this shows the following result in the F# interactive:

```
val qrlTheta : Vector<float> =
  DenseVector 5-Double
   2.57806
-0.0650069
  0.137941
-0.0064542
   1.66903
```

Now using these theta values, the predicted miles per gallon for the unknown car can be found by the following code snippet:

```
let mpgPredicted = qrlTheta * vector[8.;360.;215.;4615.;14.]
```

Similarly, SVD can be used to find the linear regression coefficients as done for QR:

```
let svdTheta = MultipleRegression.SVD( created2 ,Y_MPG)
```

Weighted linear regression

Sometimes each sample, or in other words, each row of the predictor variable matrix, is treated with different weightage. Normally, weights are given by a diagonal matrix where each element on the diagonal represent the weight for the row. If the weight is represented by W, then theta (or the linear regression coefficient) is given by the following formula:

$$\theta = \left(X'WX\right)^{-1} X'WY$$

Math.NET has a special class called `WeightedRegression` to find theta. If all the elements of the weight matrix are 1 then we have the same linear regression model as before.

The weight matrix is normally determined by taking a look at the new value for which the target variable has to be evaluated. If the new value is depicted as x, then the weights are normally calculated using the following formula:

$$W_i = \exp\left(\frac{-\left(x^i - x\right)^2}{2\tau^2}\right)$$

The numerator of the weight matrix can be calculated as the Euclidean distance between two vectors. The first vector is from the training data and the other is the new vector depicting the new entry for which the weight has to be determined.

Using the `L2Norm()` method in Math.Net, we can find this. The following code snippet shows this with a dummy matrix `m`:

```
let m = matrix[[2.;3.;4.;5.]
               [4.;55.;2.;4.]
               [3.;4.;2.;3.]
               [2.;4.;2.;1.]]


let x_n = vector[1.;2.2;31.;4.1]

//the weight matrix. The following line has to be in a single line
let W = DiagonalMatrix.ofDiagArray[|for i in 0 .. 3 -> (m.Row i).Subtract(x_n).L2Norm()|]
```

When executed in the F# interactive, this produces the following result for W:

```
val W : Matrix<float> =
  DiagonalMatrix 4x4-Double
27.0453        0        0        0
      0  60.3146        0        0
      0        0  29.1453        0
      0        0        0  29.2378
```

However, so far only the numerator of the weight matrix is calculated. Now, to calculate the denominator, you will have to experiment with several values of τ (read as "tau"). τ is called the "bandwidth" parameter.

So if we choose τ to be 1, then the weight matrix can be calculated as follows:

```
//Experiment with several values of tau
let tau = 1.
//the weight matrix
let W = DiagonalMatrix.ofDiagArray[|for i in 0 .. 3 -> (m.Row i).Subtract(x_n).L2Norm() / (2.*tau**2.)|]
```

Now we can use this technique to find the weight matrix for the miles per gallon dataset.

The following is the code that finds the predicted value of miles per gallon for the unknown car for which details were provided.

```
let unknownCarDetails = vector [4.;140.;90.;2264.;15.5]

let values = [|for i in 0 .. 349 -> (created2.Row i).Subtract(unknownCarDetails).L2Norm() / (2.*tau**2.)|]
let Weights_MPG = DiagonalMatrix.ofDiagArray values

let Theta_MPG = (created2.Transpose() * Weights_MPG  * created2).Inverse()
                * created2.Transpose() * Weights_MPG * milesPerGallon


let predictedMPG = Theta_MPG * unknownCarDetails
```

Plotting the result of multiple linear regression

Using FsPlot, I plotted the data of the cars and the miles per gallon as a scatter plot:

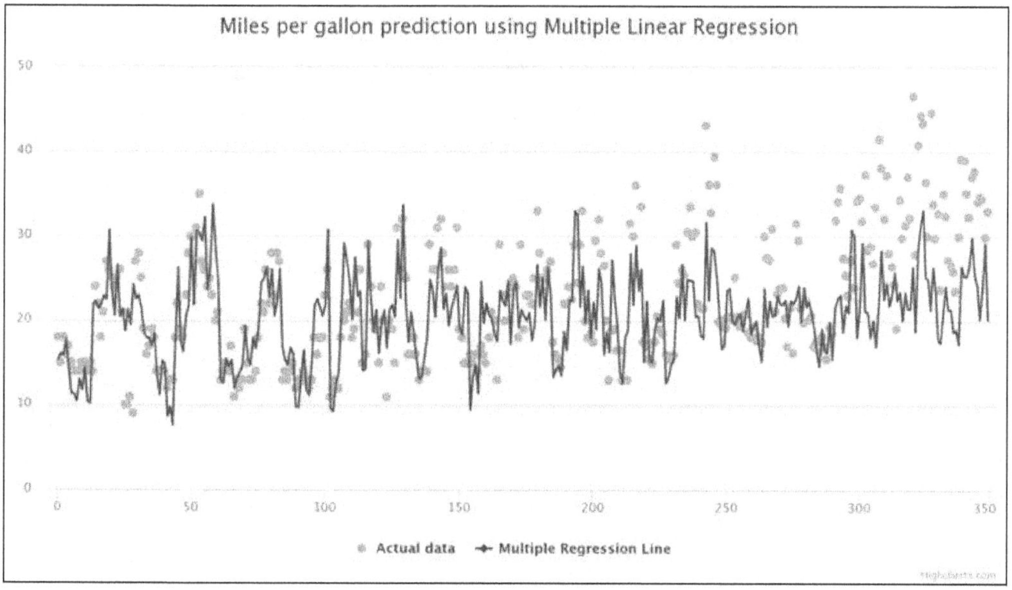

So for each data point, I plotted a dot and then plotted the predicted value of the miles per gallon (the prediction was performed using multiple linear regression).

The following code renders the chart:

```
let mpgPairs = [|for i in 0 .. 349 -> (i, milesPerGallon.At(i))|]

let predictedMPGPairs = [|for i in 0 .. 349 -> (i, Theta_MPG* created2.Row(i))|]

let scatterMPG = Series.Scatter mpgPairs

let linearRegSpline = Series.Line predictedMPGPairs

let chartMPG =
    [scatterMPG;linearRegSpline]
    |> Chart.Combine
    |> Chart.WithNames ["Actual data"; "Multiple Regression Line"]
    |> Chart.WithTitle "Miles per gallon prediction using Multiple Linear Regression"
    |> Chart.WithLegend true
```

As a measure to find out whether the model is working better or not, you can find out the average residual value. A residual is the difference between the actual value and the predicted value. So for our example of miles per gallon dataset for multiple linear regression, the average residual can be calculated as follows:

```
let mpgResiduals = [|for i in 0 .. 349 ->(milesPerGallon.At(i),
                                           Theta_MPG* created2.Row(i),
                                           milesPerGallon.At(i)-Theta_MPG* created2.Row(i))|]
                                           |> Seq.ofArray
                                           |> Seq.take 5
                                           |> Seq.toArray
```

When executed in the F# interactive, this produces the following output. To save space, I have taken only the first five rows.

```
val mpgResiduals : (float * float * float) [] =
  [|(18.0, 15.37701898, 2.622981024); (15.0, 16.05735903, -1.057359031);
    (18.0, 15.88952375, 2.110476246); (16.0, 17.78011233, -1.780112326);
    (17.0, 14.19868013, 2.801319873)|]
```

From this you can see that for the first record, the actual MPG value was 18 and the predicted value was 15.377 roughly. So the residual for this entry is about 2.623. The smaller the average residual, the better the model.

One way to see the residuals visually is to plot them as column chart. The following code generates a combination chart (shown later) to show residuals, real values, and the regression line in a single chart:

```
let mpgResidualPairs = Series.Column [|for i in 0 .. 349 -> (i,abs ( milesPerGallon.At(i) - Theta_MPG* created2.Row(i)))|]
let predictedMPGPairs = Series.Line [|for i in 0 .. 349 -> (i, Theta_MPG* created2.Row(i))|]
let actualMPGRecords = Series.Spline [|for i in 0 .. 349 -> (i, milesPerGallon.At(i))|]
let scatterMPG = Series.Scatter mpgPairs

let chartMPGResidue =
    [mpgResidualPairs;scatterMPG;predictedMPGPairs]
    |> Chart.Combine
    |> Chart.WithNames ["Residuals";"Actual data"; "Multiple Regression Line"]
    |> Chart.WithTitle "Miles per gallon prediction using Multiple Linear Regression"
    |> Chart.WithLegend true
```

This produces the following output:

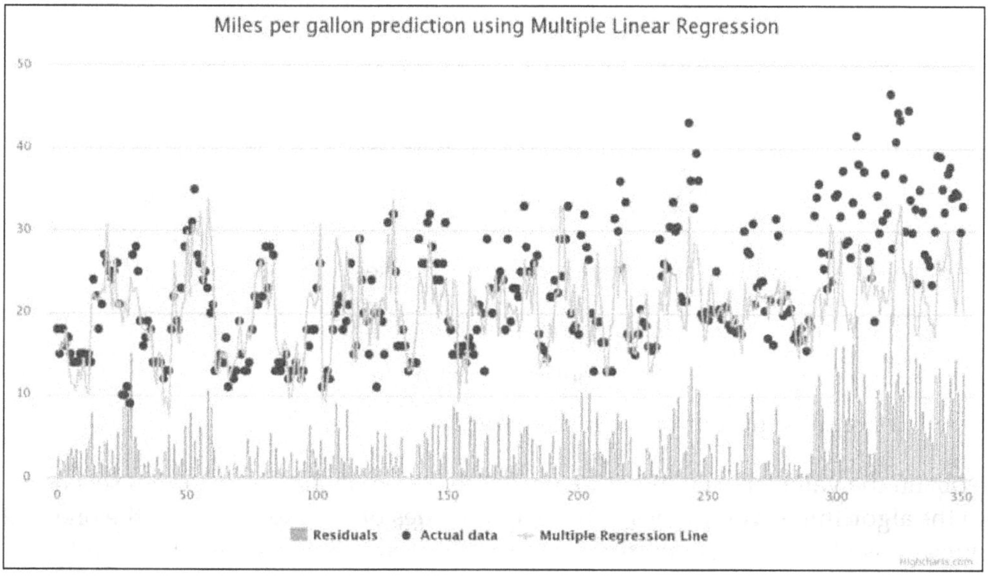

Ridge regression

Ridge regression is a technique to block the cases where X'X becomes singular. I is an identity matrix where all the elements in the diagonal are 1 and all the other elements are zero. λ is a user-defined scalar value and it is used to minimize the prediction error.

$$\theta = \left(X'X + \lambda I\right)^{-1} X'Y$$

The following code snippet uses the house price example to find the theta using ridge regression model:

```
//Let's say we have details about several houses
//With "bedrooms","Area","Bathroom" count as listed below
let houseDetails = matrix[[3.5;4000.;3.]
                          [5.;4542.;3.]
                          [3.;2545.;4.]
                          [2.;1150.;2.]
                          [2.;1220.;2.]
                          [1.;734.;1.]]

let lambda = 11.
let newHouseDetails = vector[1.;750.;1.]
let prices = vector[3400.;2102.;1334.;3432.;5342.;782.;]


let I = DenseMatrix.identity<float> houseDetails.ColumnCount

let ridgeRegressionTheta = (houseDetails.Transpose() * houseDetails
                            + lambda * I).Inverse()
                           * houseDetails.Transpose()
                           * prices
let newHousePredictedPrice = newHouseDetails * ridgeRegressionTheta
```

The price is a vector holding the price of all the houses.

- λ is known as the Shrinkage Parameter
- λ controls the size of the coefficients of theta
- λ controls the amount of regularization

To obtain the value of λ, you have to break the training data into several sets and run the algorithm several times with several values of λ, and then find the one that is most sensible and reduces error the most. There are some techniques to find the value of λ using SVD but it's not proven to work all the time.

Multivariate multiple linear regression

When you want to predict multiple target values for the same set of predictor variables, you need to use **multivariate multiple linear** regression. Multivariate linear regression takes an array of a set of predictors and an associated list of outcomes for each of this predictor set of values.

In this example, we will use Accord.NET to find the relationships between several data:

1. Get Accord Statistics via NuGet by giving the following command in PM console:

   PM> Install-Package Accord.Statistics -Version 2.15.0

2. Once you install this package, the following code finds coefficients of the multivariate linear regression for sample data:

```
//Locate these files and provide correct paths to all these files
#r @"...\packages\Accord.2.15.0\lib\net45\Accord.dll"
#r @"...\packages\Accord.Math.2.15.0\lib\net45\Accord.Math.dll"
#r @"...\packages\Accord.Statistics.2.15.0\lib\net45\Accord.Statistics.dll"
#r @"...\packages\MathNet.Numerics.FSharp.3.10.0\lib\net40\MathNet.Numerics.FSharp.dll"
#r @"...\packages\MathNet.Numerics.3.10.0\lib\net40\MathNet.Numerics.dll"
#load "...\packages\MathNet.Numerics.FSharp.3.10.0\MathNet.Numerics.fsx"

open Accord.Statistics
open Accord.Statistics.Models.Regression.Linear
open MathNet.Numerics.LinearRegression
open MathNet.Numerics.LinearAlgebra
open MathNet.Numerics.LinearAlgebra.Double
open MathNet.Numerics
//Input set of values
let inputs = [|[|1.;1.;1.|];[|2.;1.;1.|];[|3.;1.;1.|]|]
//Output for
let outputs = [|[|2.;3.|];[|4.;6.|];[|6.;9.|]|]
//This is a regression that takes a input variable set of 3
values
//each and projects the result to a two variable output.
//Thus we need a 3 x 2 regression model
let regression = new MultivariateLinearRegression (3, 2);

let error = regression.Regress (inputs, outputs)

printfn "%A" regression.Coefficients
//Let's say we have a new set of values as per the given data
let newInput = DenseMatrix.OfColumns [[2.4;1.2;1.4]]
//Creating a theta from this coefficinets
let theta = DenseMatrix.OfArray regression.Coefficients
//Calculating the predicted value for this new input set.
let newOutputs = theta.Transpose() * newInput
```

Feature scaling

If your features for linear regression are in different ranges, the result produced can be skewed. For example, if one of the features is in the range of 1 to 10 and the other is in the range of 3,000 to 50,000, then the predicted model will be bad. In such cases, the features must be rescaled so that they belong to almost the same range—ideally between 0 and 1.

The common strategy to scale a feature is to find the average and the range, and then using the following formula, all the values are updated:

$$x_i = \frac{x_i - \mu}{S}$$

In the preceding formula, μ is the mean or average of the values of feature x and S is the range or the standard deviation. The following code snippet shows how you can perform a feature scaling using F#.

You can calculate the feature scaling features by hand like this and then update the predictor matrix manually.

```
//feature scaling
let avgBedRooms =  houseDetails.Column 0 |> Seq.average
let avgArea =  houseDetails.Column 1 |> Seq.average
let avgBathRooms =  houseDetails.Column 2 |> Seq.average
let rangeBedRooms =  (houseDetails.Column 0 |> Seq.max) - (houseDetails.Column 0 |> Seq.min)
let rangeArea =  (houseDetails.Column 1 |> Seq.max) - (houseDetails.Column 1 |> Seq.min)
let rangeBathRooms =  (houseDetails.Column 2 |> Seq.max) - (houseDetails.Column 2 |> Seq.min)

//However, you can't do this for a very large matrix.
//So the following code does that programmatically for matrix of any size:

//This method performs feature scaling for all the columns
let scaleFeatures (avgs: float []) (ranges: float [])  (column : Vector<float>) =
    for i in 0 .. avgs.Length - 1   do
        column.Storage.At(i,(column.Storage.At(i)- avgs.[i])/ranges.[i])
    column

//Finding averages for all columns
let allAvgs = [|for i in 0 .. houseDetails.ColumnCount - 1
                -> houseDetails.Column i |> Seq.average|]
//Finding ranges for all columns
let allRanges = [|for i in 0 .. houseDetails.ColumnCount - 1 ->
                  (houseDetails.Column i |> Seq.max) - (houseDetails.Column i |> Seq.min)|]
let allColumns = [for i in 0 .. houseDetails.ColumnCount - 1 ->
                  (houseDetails.Column i) ]

//Scaled Column values
let scaledColumns = allColumns
                    |> List.map ( fun column -> scaleFeatures allAvgs allRanges column)
//Creating a matrix from scaled values.
let scaledHouseDetails = DenseMatrix.ofColumns scaledColumns
```

After the scaling, the house details matrix looks like this:

```
val it : Matrix<float> =
  DenseMatrix 6x3-Double
   0.1875    999.313      0.0625
-0.619792  0.571647  -0.620317
 0.166667     847.5         0.5
        2      1150           2
        2      1220           2
        1       734           1
```

These values of the scaled matrix are very close to each other and thus the linear model generated.

Summary

In this chapter, you learned about several linear regression models. I hope you will find this information useful to solve some of your own practical problems. For example, you can predict your next electrical bill by doing a historical survey of your old bills. When not sure, start with a single predictor and gradually add more predictors to find a suitable model. Also, you can ask domain experts to locate predictor variables. Although there can be a temptation to use linear regression for prediction, don't give in. Linear regression can't work that way.

In the next chapter, you will learn about several supervised learning algorithms for classification. I hope you have enjoyed reading this chapter.

3
Classification Techniques

"Telling chalk and cheese apart"

In the previous chapter, you learned how to predict the real values using linear regression. In this chapter, you will learn about classification. Classification is the process of tagging/marking a given object with a class/tag value. For example, for a given set of cancer patient records with benign and malignant cancerous cases, a program can be written to automatically categorize the new patient record to be either benign or malignant.

What's fascinating about this approach is that the algorithm doesn't change and you can use the same algorithm to predict other things that are important in other settings. For example, the same algorithm can tell apart dogs and cats from their photographs, as you will find out later in the chapter.

In this chapter, you will learn how to implement several algorithms in F# that are used for classification. For some simple algorithms, such as k-NN, you will develop the algorithm from scratch using F#, but for more involved ones, you will learn how to use a mature and robust industry standard machine learning framework, such as Accord.NET and Weka (through WekaSharp).

Objective

After reading this chapter, you will be able to break down a real problem to a classification problem whenever applicable and then be able to use the proper algorithm to solve the problem.

Different classification algorithms you will learn

Following are the different types of algorithms that you will be looking into:

- k-NN (K Nearest Neighbor)
- Logistic regression
- Multinomial logistic regression
- Decision trees (J48)

Some interesting things you can do

You can use machine learning to differentiate between dogs and cats from photographs. Then surprisingly enough, you may tweak the same algorithm to detect the cancerous cells from the normal cells in breast cancer patients. You may use decision trees to predict whether there will be a traffic jam on a given date and time. There can be several other parameters that can be helpful while predicting a traffic jam. The intention is that after reading this chapter you will be able to use these classification techniques to address some of the problems you are facing yourself.

Binary classification using k-NN

In this example, you will solve the kaggle cat and dog identification challenge (`https://www.kaggle.com/c/dogs-vs-cats`). The challenge is to identify dogs and cats from photographs. Following are a couple of example photographs:

- Image 1

- Image 2

How might we decide if an image contains a cat or a dog? What are the visual differences between cats and dogs? Some of these might be difficult. For example, detecting the lengths of their whiskers is hard for a computer, because the whiskers are small in the images. What about color? It seems promising!

Cats and dogs have very different textures. They have distinctly different colored furs and also the textures of the furs are different. Also, the dogs have a bigger darker nose while the cats mostly have lighter colored skin around their nose. The dogs have much bigger eyes than the cats. Bigger eyes and darker noses contribute to the fact that a photograph of a dog has to be darker in general as compared to that of a cat. However, this hypothesis will be ruled out if we have a black cat and a white dog. Leaving out those extreme cases, this seems to be a good start in an attempt to figure out whether the photograph is that of a cat or a dog. We can build a nearest neighbor learning algorithm model based on this hypothesis.

This means that if we can create a histogram of the colors available in the photographs of dogs and cats, then we can probably predict whether the photograph has the picture of a feline or a canine. The preceding two photographs were taken from the cats and dogs challenge dataset. The cat image is `cat.456.jpg` and the dog image is `dog.4.jpg`. These two photographs will be used as test cases of the program. You can get these images from `https://www.kaggle.com/c/dogs-vs-cats/data` inside the train folder.

In this section, you will see how you can use k-NN to classify dogs and cats. The following F# application does this job:

```
open System
open System.IO
open System.Drawing

type Entry = {Label :string; Values : float []}

//Gets the histogram from the pixel values
let getHist (values: float[]) =
    values |> Seq.groupBy ( fun color -> color)
           |> Map.ofSeq
           |> Map.map (fun t colors -> Seq.length colors)
           |> Map.toArray
           |> Array.map ( fun colorCount ->  float (snd  colorCount))
```

```
//Getting pixel values from the image
let getImageAsArray (fileName:string) =
     let img = Image.FromFile fileName
     let ms = new MemoryStream()
     img.Save (ms, System.Drawing.Imaging.ImageFormat.Jpeg)
     ms.ToArray() |> Array.map ( fun t -> float t)
```

```
//Adjusted Euclidean distance: Calculates the Euclidean distance between two vectors
//as long as the values are present in both the vectors. This works even when the
//vectors are of different lengths.
let distance ( values1 : float []  , values2 : float []) =
    let v1length = values1.Length
    let v2length = values2.Length
    let mL = min v1length v2length
    let v1s = values1 |> Seq.take mL |> Seq.toArray
    let v2s = values2 |> Seq.take mL |> Seq.toArray
    v1s |> Array.zip v2s
        |> Array.map (fun t -> float ( fst t) - float ( snd t))
        |> Array.map (fun t -> t ** 2.)
        |> Array.sum
```

```
//k-Nearest Neighbor
let kNN ( entries : Entry list, newEntry : string * float[] , k : int) =
 entries  |> List.map( fun x -> ( x.Label, distance  (x.Values, snd (newEntry))))
          |> List.sortBy snd
          |> Seq.ofList
          |> Seq.take k
          |> Seq.countBy fst
          |> Seq.toList
```

```
let knownDog = getHist ( getImageAsArray "dog.4.jpg")
let knownCat = getHist ( getImageAsArray "cat.456.jpg")
//Load values from training images.
let loaded = Directory.GetFiles("Dogs and Cats/train")
                      |> Array.map ( fun t -> new FileInfo(t))
                      |> Array.toSeq
                      |> Seq.map (fun t ->
             {
                 Label = t.Name.Substring(0,3);
                 Values = getHist (getImageAsArray t.FullName)
             })
            |> Seq.toList
```

```
let unknownEntry1 = ("X",knownDog)
let unknownEntry2 = ("X",knownCat)
//Let's consider only 5 nearest neighbors
let k = 5
//Getting back the labels for each of the nearest neighbours
let labels1 = kNN (loaded , unknownEntry1, k)
printfn "%A" labels1
//Locating the guess. The one with the maximum votes
let guess1 = fst(  labels1 |> List.item 0)
printfn "The known dog is identified as a %A" guess1
//Getting back the labels for each of the nearest neighbours
let labels2 = kNN (loaded , unknownEntry2, k)
printfn "%A" labels2
//Locating the guess. The one with the maximum votes
let guess2 = fst(  labels2 |> List.item 0)
printfn "The known cat is identified as a %A" guess2
```

This produces the following output:

```
[("dog", 4); ("cat", 1)]
The known dog is identified as a "dog"
[("cat", 3); ("dog", 2)]
The known cat is identified as a "cat"
```

How does it work?

Since the images are of different sizes, I decided to create a histogram of color values. There is a maximum of 256 color shades. So each image can be represented as an entry with an array of 256 or less (some images have less colors than others) float values representing the number of times each color occurred in the image and the class of the image. In this case, the class is either "dog" or "cat".

The function distance(`values1:float[],values2:float[]`) calculates the Euclidean distance between two images. This means that this function uses the histograms of colors for these two images and then finds the distance between these two images as if they are represented in the N dimension by these two arrays, `values1` and `values2`. Since the images are of different sizes, this function finds the minimum length and calculates the distance till that index. Images that are similar will be represented by points which are closer to each other.

At the heart of this solution is the following function which implements the k-NN model:

```
let kNN ( entries : Entry list, newEntry : string * float[] , k : int)
```

It takes the list of entries that represent the class/tag of the image and the list of float values that represent the image. The `newEntry` is the image that needs to be classified; so it is represented as a tuple of string and a float array. `k` is an integer that represents how many nearest neighbors need to be considered before getting to a conclusion about the new image represented by `newEntry`. Typical values of `k` are 3 and 5.

Finding cancerous cells using k-NN: a case study

The same algorithm, without any change, can be used to differentiate between the cancerous cells and the normal ones. You can download a list of breast cancer cell data from `https://archive.ics.uci.edu/ml/machine-learning-databases/breast-cancer-wisconsin/wdbc.data`. The second column represents whether the cell is cancerous or not. If it is cancerous then the mark is **M**, else it is **B**.

The first few columns of the first couple of rows are shown next:

```
842302,M,17.99,10.38,122.8,1001,0.1184,0.2776,0.3001,0.1471,0.2
842517,M,20.57,17.77,132.9,1326,0.08474,0.07864,0.0869,0.07017,
```

The first column is the ID and the second column is the class that represents whether the person has cancer or not (M or B— "M" is short for "Malignant" and "B" is short for "Benign").

So you see that each row can be modeled with the following type, as done for the previous example:

```
type Entry = {Label :string; Values : float []}
```

So if all the data is loaded and fed to the same algorithm, we can predict the possible class of an unseen entry to be either M or B.

```
//Loading all the breast cancer data in a strongly typed list of Entry
//representing each row of the breast cancer database
let parseLine (line:string) =
        let toks = line.Split ','
        (
            {
                Label =  toks.[1];
                Values = toks.[2..]|> Seq.map ( fun f -> float f) |> Seq.toArray
            }
        )
```

Generally, a 70-20-10% split scheme is used to generate the training, cross validation, and test data from the given training corpus. The following code snippets generate the training, cross validation, and test set from the given training corpus. I have saved the data locally in the `wdbc.data` file.

- **Training data**: This is used to train your machine learning algorithm.
- **Test data**: This is used to find the result of the algorithm. For best results, the amount of overlap between the training data and the test data should be minimal. Otherwise, if the training data looks almost like the test data then the algorithm will almost always generate the correct result and this will lead to false confidence that it (the algorithm) is getting better.

- **Cross validation data**: This is the data set that is (part of the test data) to be used to validate the result. If the algorithm fails to do well with the cross validation data fed as test data, then it has to be fixed.

```
let cancerData = System.IO.File.ReadLines  @"wdbc.data" |> Seq.map parseLine
//Finding total number or entries
let ll =  float (cancerData |> Seq.length)
//Allocating 70% as the training example
let trainingSampleCount = int ( floor( (70. * ll )/100.))
//Allocating 20% as the cross validation samples
let crossValidationSampleCount = int ( floor( (20. * ll )/100.))
//Leaving the rest of the examples as test samples
let testSampleCount = int ll - trainingSampleCount-crossValidationSampleCount
//Total number of training and cross validation examples
let totalTraining = trainingSampleCount + crossValidationSampleCount
//Training corpus
let trainingCorpus = cancerData |> Seq.take trainingSampleCount |> Seq.toList
//Cross validation corpus
let crossValidation = cancerData |> Seq.skip trainingSampleCount |> Seq.take crossValidationSampleCount
//Test corpus
let testCorpus = cancerData |> Seq.skip  totalTraining |> Seq.take testSampleCount
```

At this point you can use the algorithm to find the predicted class of an entry from the test corpus. Here I have taken an example, which is of type M:

```
//Predict the class of this patient record
let unknown = ("X",[|20.92;25.09;143.;1347.;0.1099;0.2236;0.3174;0.1474;0.2149;0.06879;
                      0.9622;1.026;8.758;118.8;0.006399;0.0431;0.07845;0.02624;0.02057;0.006213;
                      24.29;29.41;179.1;1819.;0.1407;0.4186;0.6599;0.2542;0.2929;0.09873|])
let K = 10
let labels = kNN (trainingCorpus, unknown , K)
printfn "%A" labels
```

This prints the following output at the F# interactive:

```
val labels : (string * int) list = [("M", 10)]
```

This means that all the `10` nearest neighbors are of type M. Thus, this unseen entry will be tagged with class M. Now let's see how the code performs for `k = 10` in cross validation and test corpus on a whole. The following code finds that out:

```
//Finds the accuracy of the kNN model for the given test corpus
//and for the given value of k
let findAccuracyOf ( entries: Entry list) (trainingCorpus: Entry list) (k : int) =
    let totalCount = entries |> List.length
    //How many entries were recognized correctly.
    let correctCount = entries
                        |> List.countBy (fun t -> t.Label = fst (kNN ( trainingCorpus,("X", t.Values), k)
                                                               |> List.toArray).[0])
                        |> List.filter ( fun item -> fst item = true)
                        |> List.map ( fun item -> snd item)
                        |> List.sum
    //Returns the percentage which is recognized correctly.
    float correctCount / float totalCount
```

Use this code to find the percentage of entries from the test corpus which are recognized correctly:

```
findAccuracyOf (testCorpus |> Seq.toList ) 10
```

This produces the following output in the F# interactive when run in the interactive:

```
val it : float = 0.9137931034
```

That means roughly 91.38% of the entries were diagnosed correctly using K-NN. Not bad for an algorithm finding cancerous cells. Unfortunately, this is the optimal performance you will get should you use all the parameters. The lowest value of `k` that you can use (which you shouldn't ideally) is 1. And for even `k = 1` the recognized entries plateau is at 91.38%. This is sometimes referred to as the curse of dimensionality. There are 30 values associated with each entry. So essentially we are finding the distance between two points in 30 dimensions. If you can reduce this dimension, you might get a boost in the performance of the prediction. However, I will leave that as an exercise for you to do experimentation on.

Understanding logistic regression

Unlike linear regression which is used to predict the real values of a real entity, logistic regression is used to predict the class or tag of an unseen entry. Logistic regression's output is either a 0 or a 1 depicting the predicted class of the unseen entry. Logistic regression uses a smooth curve whose values range from 0 to 1 for all the values of the independent variable.

Sigmoid function (also called logistic function) is one option for this function. This is defined by the following formula:

$$g(z) = \frac{1}{\left(1+e^{-z}\right)}$$

The sigmoid function chart

The following chart is generated by the code snippet using FsPlot:

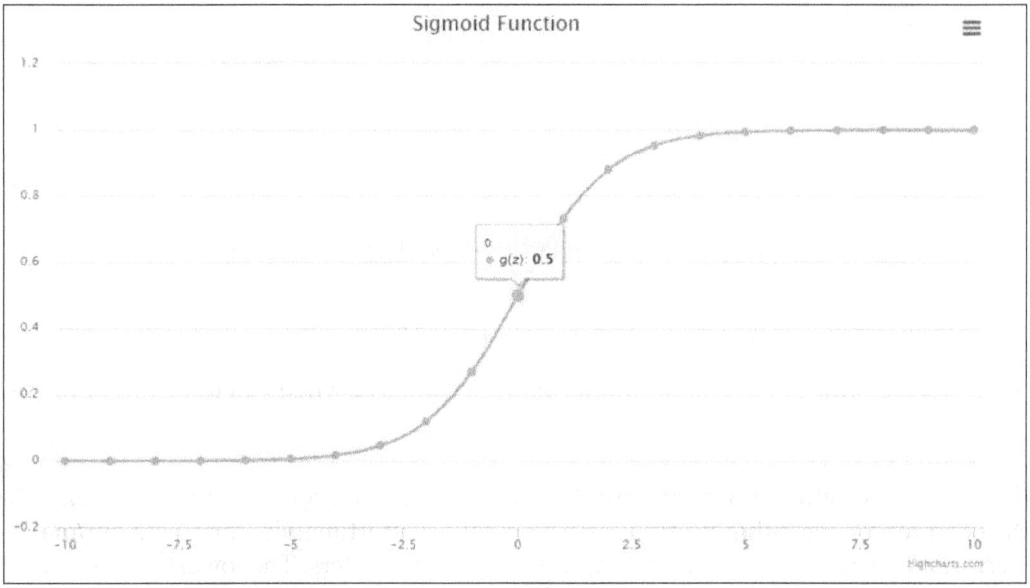

You need to install Chrome to get the chart rendered.

```
#load @"...\packages\FsPlot.0.6.6\FsPlotBootstrap.fsx"
open FsPlot.Highcharts.Charting

//Logistic Regression
let z = [for i in -10. .. 10. -> (i,1./(1.+exp -i))]
z
 |> Chart.Spline
 |> Chart.WithTitle "Sigmoid Function"
 |> Chart.WithName "g(z)"
```

So you see that the function value approaches 1 as the value of X approaches infinity, and it approaches 0 as the value of X approaches negative infinity. So for any given value of X, you can determine the class if you set your threshold at 0.5. In other words, you can say that if for a given value of X the value of the sigmoid function is more than 0.5, then you can train your logistic regression model to emit that the class of X is 1 else the class in which X belongs is 0.

So the hypothesis for logistic regression is governed by the following equation:

$$h_\theta(x) = g\left(\theta^T x\right) = \frac{1}{\left(1 + e^{-\theta^T x}\right)}$$

Theta is the parameter to be learnt by the model to predict the class of a new entry. The following code snippet shows how logistic regression can be used to do binary classification. This example creates the model from scratch.

```
#load @"...\packages\MathNet.Numerics.FSharp.3.10.0\MathNet.Numerics.fsx"
open MathNet.Numerics.LinearAlgebra
//Dummy data representing some attribute values about some entity.
let X = matrix [[1. ;2.; 3.;2.]
                [4. ;5.; 2.;1.]
                [7. ;0.8; 9.;1.3]
                [11.;1.1;21.;1.]]
//Their corresponding classes/categories/tags
let Y = matrix[[0.]
               [0.]
               [0.]
               [1.]]
//Learning rate (or the rate of convergence to a terminal value of
//theta. This is the rate of convergence towards the solution.
let alpha = 0.25
```

```
//Number of examples
let m = 4.0
//Gets the histogram from the pixel values
let theta = matrix [[0.]
                    [0.]
                    [0.]
                    [0.]]
//The sigmoid function
let sigmoid x = 1./(1. + exp -x)
//Calculating the value of the hypothesis
let h = theta.Transpose() * X |> Matrix.map ( fun t -> sigmoid t)
//Calculating the updated value of theta
let thetaM = theta - alpha/m*(X.Transpose()*(h.Transpose()-Y))
//Here is an unknown/new entry for which we have to determine the class
let unknownX = vector [12.;3.;24.;6.]
//Here is the predicted value of the logistic (a.k.a logit model)
let predictionLR =  thetaM.Transpose() * unknownX
//Calculating the log likelihood
//pR stands for prediction
let pR  = log10 (abs( predictionLR.At 0))
```

When run, this produces the following output:

```
val predictionLR : Vector<float> = DenseVector 1-Double
3.62813

val pR : float = 0.5596822414
```

Since the value of `pR` is more than 0.5, the predicted class of this unseen entry will be 1. Now looking back at the training data, it makes more sense. If you look at the training data, you will see that the last example of the training dataset is close to the unknown entry and it also belongs to class "1".

Now if you change the unknown entry attributes to the following and run the code again, you will get a different value of `pR`:

```
let unknownX = vector [1.23;3.12;2.21;1.56]
```

In this case, the value of `pR` will be less than 0.5, as shown next:

```
val pR : float = -0.43282654
```

Thus, you can determine the class of this entry to be "0" and this also is aligned with the training data, because if you look at the training data you will see that the entries close to the unknown X entry belong to class "0".

Theta is updated by the following rule:

$$\theta_m = \theta - (\alpha / m) * \left(X^T * \left(h^T - Y\right)\right)$$

α is the learning rate and m is the number of records in the training data.

The predicted class can be found by multiplying the values of theta with the unknown X:

$$Prediction = \theta^T * X_{unknown}$$

The value for `thetaM` from the last example is seen:

```
val thetaM : Matrix<float> =
  DenseMatrix 4x1-Double
 -0.03125
-0.209375
  0.21875
-0.103125
```

In the next section, you will learn how to use Accord.NET for logistic regression calculation. We will use the same cats and dogs dataset to showcase how the logistic regression model (sometimes also referred to as the logit model) can be used to identify dogs and cats.

Binary classification using logistic regression (using Accord.NET)

Using logistic regression we can also classify the cats and the dogs. The hypothesis is that the photograph of a dog will generally have more black than that of a cat, unless we are dealing with photographs of black cats. This is so because the dogs have much bigger eyes which are black and a much darker and bigger (generally black) noses than the domestic feline members.

Following is the code that uses Accord.NET for logistic regression to use this model to tell dogs and cats apart. There are two inputs to the model: the average pixel value and the percentage of black color in the photograph. The model to be implemented using Accord.NET takes a set of inputs and a set of labels. Although the datatype of labels is `float`, don't get fooled by thinking that they can be real valued in the continuous range. They have to be discreet.

In this case, I have mapped the "dog" class to be 1.0 and the "cat" class to be 0.0.

```
#r @"...\packages\Accord.Statistics.3.0.2\lib\net45\Accord.Statistics.dll"
open Accord.Statistics
//Learns the model using Accord.Statistics.Models.Regression.LogisticRegression
let learnModel ( inputs : float [] []) (labels : float []) =
  let lr =  new Accord.Statistics.Models.Regression.LogisticRegression 2
  let teacher = new Accord.Statistics.Models.Regression.Fitting.IterativeReweightedLeastSquares(lr)
  let mutable delta = 0.0;
  let mutable continueLooping = true
  while continueLooping do
    delta <- teacher.Run( inputs, labels )
    if delta <= 0.001 then continueLooping <- false
  lr
```

```
//Creates an entry based on the model
let createModelEntry (fileName: string) =
    let values = getImageAsArray fileName
    let mutable label = 0.
    if fileName.Contains "dog" then  label <- 1. else label <- 0.
    let avg = values |> Array.average
    let blackPercentage = float  (values|> Array.filter ( fun t -> t = 0.0)
                                         |> Array.length)/ float (values.Length)
    (label,[|avg; blackPercentage|])
```

```
//Loads the data using
let createIOCombo (dir:string) =
    Directory.GetFiles(dir)
            |> Seq.map createModelEntry
            |> Seq.toList
```

Using it from the `Main` method is simple.

```
//Load values
let knownCatVals = snd (createModelEntry "cat.456.jpg")
//Change the path to point to your disk
let combo = createIOCombo @"C:\Dogs and Cats\train" |> Seq.take 10
let labels = combo |> Seq.map fst |> Seq.toArray
printfn "%A" labels
let inputs = combo |> Seq.map snd |> Seq.toArray
printfn "%A" inputs
let lr = learnModel inputs labels
printfn "%A" lr
let isCat = lr.Compute (knownCatVals)
printfn "%A" isCat
```

This produces the following output:

```
val labels : float [] = [|0.0; 0.0; 0.0; 0.0; 0.0; 0.0; 0.0; 0.0; 0.0;
0.0|]
val inputs : float [] [] =
  [|[|117.30232; 0.01047204769|]; [|124.6393365; 0.01238151659|];
    [|124.9631939; 0.006673466414|]; [|123.7237904; 0.00916234979|];
    [|124.7680013; 0.01430013459|]; [|126.4313708; 0.01207619395|];
    [|123.9840788; 0.01101676305|]; [|119.6161412; 0.01348987288|];
    [|124.1002675; 0.01194934903|]; [|124.2808911; 0.01125414322|]|]
val lr : LogisticRegression
val isCat : float = 1.0
```

This means that the program has identified the photograph as that of a cat. However, this may be a very bad model to try to recognize cats and dogs based on the darkness of the photograph. But I hope you get the point of how to use logistic regression to classify. Our logit model here is limited to two input parameters: the average pixel value and the amount of darkness. These two parameters are referred to as features.

In the next example you will see how to use logistic regression to determine the class of multiple types using the one-vs-all method.

Multiclass classification using logistic regression

You have seen in the previous section how logistic regression can be used to perform binary classification. In this section, you will see how to use logistic regression (which is known to do the binary classification) for multiclass classification. The algorithm used is known as the "one-vs-all" method.

The algorithm is very intuitive. It learns many models as many different classes of items are there in the training dataset. Later, when a new entry is given for identification, all the models are used to compute the confidence score that reflects the confidence of the model that the new entry belongs to that class. The model with the highest confidence is selected.

In this example, you will see how Accord.NET can be used to implement multiclass classification to identify iris flowers. There are three types of iris flowers, namely, **Iris versicolor**, **Iris setosa**, and **Iris virginica**. The task is to identify a given flower from the measurements of a few attributes, such as SepalLength, SepalWidth, PetalLength, and PetalWidth.

Following are the photos of these flowers:

- **Iris versicolor**

- **Iris virginica**

- **Iris setosa**

So the three models will be learnt from the training corpus and given unseen flower details. Each of these models will then emit a confidence score that is a measure of what the model thinks the flower is. We will select the result of the model which has the highest confidence score.

Here this algorithm is being used to identify Iris flowers:

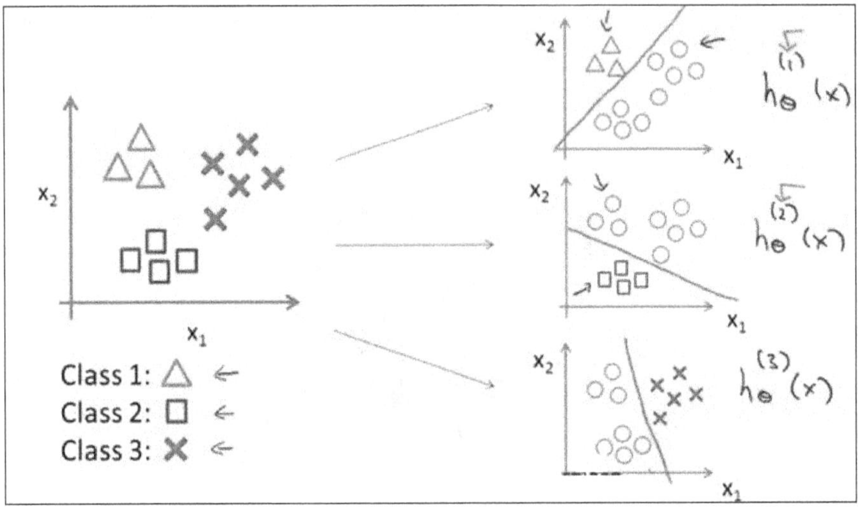

I have taken this image from professor. Andrew Ng's MOOC at `https://www.coursera.org/learn/machine-learning`.

This preceding image shows how logistic regression learns several models in the one-vs-all method to predict the class of an unseen entry.

```
/// Identifying Iris flowers using Multiclass Logistic Regression
type IrisEntry = {
                    SepalLength:float;
                    SepalWidth:float;
                    PetalLength:float;
                    PetalWidth:float;
                    Name:int
                 }
// Create a estimation algorithm to estimate the regression
let classes = [|"Iris-setosa";"Iris-versicolor";"Iris-virginica"|]
```

```
//Getting the data
let getData (fileName: string) =
    let allLines = File.ReadLines fileName
    allLines |> Seq.map ( fun line -> line.Split (','))
             |> Seq.map (fun t ->
   {
             SepalLength= float t.[0];
             SepalWidth = float  t.[1];
             PetalLength = float t.[2];
             PetalWidth = float t.[3];
             Name = Array.IndexOf (classes,  t.[4].Trim('"'));
   })
   |> Seq.map ( fun t ->
             ([|t.SepalLength;t.SepalWidth;t.PetalLength;t.PetalWidth|],t.Name))
   |> Seq.toList
```

```
//learning the model using Accord.NET
let learnTheModel (inputs:float [][]) (labels : int[]) =
 //There are 4 independent variables and 3 distinct classes
 //So we need a multinomial regression model with 4 input and 3 output classes
 let mlr = new Accord.Statistics.Models.Regression.MultinomialLogisticRegression (4, 3)
 //Create a estimation algorithm to estimate the regression
 let lbnr = new Accord.Statistics.Models.Regression.Fitting.LowerBoundNewtonRaphson(mlr)
 let mutable delta = 0.0
 let mutable iteration = 0
 let mutable continueLooping = true
 while continueLooping do
    delta <- lbnr.Run(inputs, labels)
    iteration <- iteration + 1
    if iteration > 100 || delta < 0.001 then continueLooping <- false
 mlr
```

```
let iris = getData @"C:\iris.csv"
let flowerData = iris |> List.map (fun t -> fst t) |> Seq.toArray
let flowerNames = iris |> List.map (fun t -> snd t) |> Seq.toArray
let model  = learnTheModel flowerData flowerNames
printfn "%A" (model.Compute flowerData.[100])
```

This code will produce the following output:

```
[|1.068338871e-05; 0.003554077494; 0.9964352391|]
```

This means that the model that has the highest confidence is an Iris virginica. Because the third number is close to 1 while others are almost 0. And if you look at the training data you will discover that the 100th flower in the training dataset is indeed an `"Iris-verginica"`.

However, generating the confidence scores of the model is not enough because every model developed has to be tested for accuracy. The following code finds the accuracy of the model. At first it shuffles the data to get enough of all the different types of flowers in the training dataset and then uses the cross validation and test set, which are split at 70%, 20%, and 10% respectively to find the accuracy of the model.

```
//Checking accuracy of iris flower identification systems
let getIndexOfMax (values:float []) =
    let mx = values |> Array.max
    System.Array.IndexOf (values,mx)

let getAccuracyFor( values: ( float [] * int ) list)
                  (lr:Accord.Statistics.Models.Regression.MultinomialLogisticRegression) =
    let all = values |> List.filter (fun item -> getIndexOfMax (lr.Compute(fst item)) = snd item)
    float all.Length / float values.Length
```

This means that almost 96% of the flowers were identified correctly. Not bad for a learning model!

How does it work?

The model returns confidence scores for all the learnt models, such as the following one:

```
[|1.068338871e-05; 0.003554077494; 0.9964352391|]
```

The class, however, is determined by the index of the maximum value in the array that stores the confidence of each model. The `getIndexOfMax (values:float [])` function does that for us. If you see, the third number `0.9964352391` is close to 1 while the others are almost zero. So this array can be perceived as `[|0;0;1|]`.

The following function calculates the accuracy of the prediction for the given dataset:

```
getAccuracyFor( values:( float [] * int ) list)
(lr:MultinomialLogisticRegression)
```

The following code snippet finds the entries that were identified:

```
List.filter (fun item -> getIndexOfMax (lr.Compute(fst item)) = snd
item)
```

K-NN works well when you have many degrees of freedom (or in other words, many attributes that determine the class of the target variable). Logistic regression works well when there are only a handful of attributes but a lot of rows in the training data. However, logistic regression doesn't work well on categorical attribute data. When you have a lot of categorical data in the attributes or in the predictor variable, you should consider using decision trees.

Multiclass classification using decision trees

In *Chapter 1, Introduction to Machine Learning*, you saw how decision trees work to find several classes among unseen datasets. In the following section, you will see how to use WekaSharp, which is a wrapper on top of Weka to be used in a F# friendly way. Weka is an open source project for data mining and machine learning, written in Java (`http://www.cs.waikato.ac.nz/ml/weka/`).

Obtaining and using WekaSharp

You can download WekaSharp from `https://wekasharp.codeplex.com/`. Then you have to add the following DLLs in your F# application, as shown next:

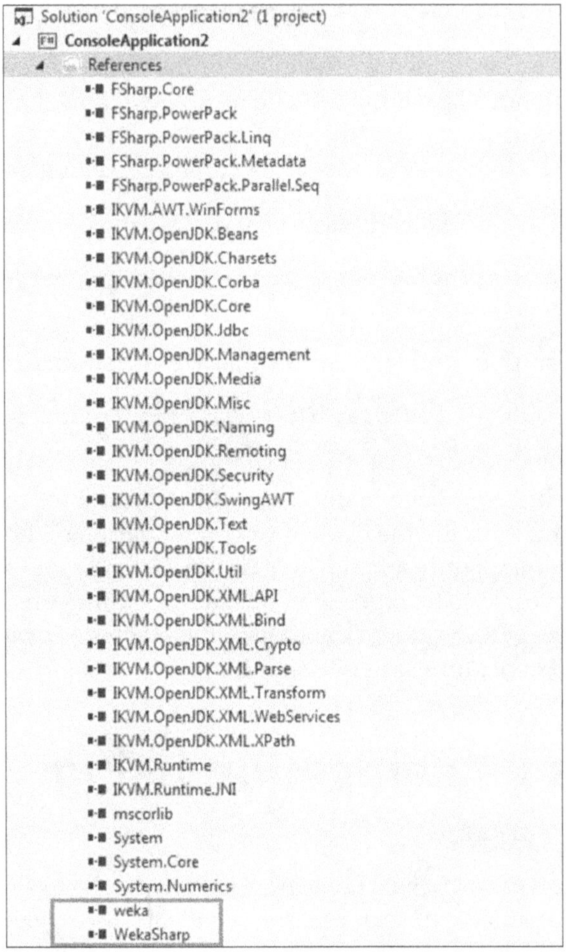

In this example, you will see how to use WekaSharp to classify the iris flowers.

```
module DecisionTreesByWeka.Main

open System
open WekaSharp.Common
open WekaSharp.Classify
open WekaSharp.Dataset
```

```
open WekaSharp.Eval


[<EntryPoint>]
let main args =
    let iris =
            @"C:\iris.csv"
            |> WekaSharp.Dataset.readArff
            |> WekaSharp.Dataset.setClassIndexWithLastAttribute

    let classes = iris.numClasses()
    printfn "%A" classes



    let j48Tt = TrainTest(iris, iris, ClassifierType.J48, WekaSharp.
Parameter.J48.DefaultPara)
    let j48Cv = CrossValidation(5, iris, ClassifierType.J48,
                            WekaSharp.Parameter.J48.DefaultPara)
    let j48Rs = RandomSplit(0.7, iris, ClassifierType.J48,
                            WekaSharp.Parameter.J48.DefaultPara)

    // perform the task and get result
    let ttAccuracy = j48Tt |> WekaSharp.Eval.evalClassify |>
WekaSharp.Eval.getAccuracy
    let cvAccuracy = j48Cv |> WekaSharp.Eval.evalClassify |>
WekaSharp.Eval.getAccuracy
    let rsAccuracy = j48Rs |> WekaSharp.Eval.evalClassify |>
WekaSharp.Eval.getAccuracy

    printfn "%A" ttAccuracy
    printfn "%A" cvAccuracy
    printfn "%A" rsAccuracy

    0
```

When we run this, it produces the following output:

```
3
97.98657718
94.63087248
93.33333333
```

This means that the classification accuracy of the decision tree is around 93%.

How does it work?

Following are the first few rows of the table (`iris.csv`):

```
sepal length,sepal width,petal length,petal width,species
5.1,3.5,1.4,0.2,Iris-setosa
4.9,3.0,1.4,0.2,Iris-setosa
4.7,3.2,1.3,0.2,Iris-setosa
4.6,3.1,1.5,0.2,Iris-setosa
```

The variable `iris` holds the data from the table (`iris.csv`). The last column is the class/tag which specifies the species of the flower. The `numClasses()` method returns the number of classes.

The following line creates a model where the entire data is supplied as the training and test data, and the J48 decision tree is used:

```
let j48Tt = TrainTest(iris, iris, ClassifierType.J48,
WekaSharp.Parameter.J48.DefaultPara)
```

The following line evaluates the model's classification for the training set and calculates the accuracy for the model; that is, it calculates how many instances from the given test data were identified correctly:

```
let ttAccuracy = j48Tt |> WekaSharp.Eval.evalClassify |>
WekaSharp.Eval.getAccuracy
```

Predicting a traffic jam using a decision tree: a case study

When I go home from the office, I face a traffic jam, as shown in the following image, as many other commuters in Bangalore do almost every day.

I thought if I could only predict a traffic jam, I would reach home early to play with my son. I observed that if it rains and if it is a weekday and if it is past 4:30 PM in the dial, a traffic jam is highly likely.

So I thought I could use a decision tree to predict whether there will be a traffic jam today or not. In the following example, I used a toy dataset that I fabricated. In the real settings, the data has to be filled following a month or few months' observations, because anomalies do exist. Sometimes, even if it rains and even if it is a weekday, there is no traffic jam. The reason may be that there is a cricket match that people want to watch and they have taken a day off work or are working from home. However, these sorts of situations are not common and shouldn't be considered as a rule.

Following are the major features that decide whether there will be a traffic jam or not:

- Is it raining?
- Is it a workday?
- Is it rush hour ?
- What time is it now?

Following are some rows of the fabricated dataset. The time is in mentioned during the afternoon; where `507` means 5:07 PM.

```
rain_chance,rush_hour,weekday,time,traffic
0.142727454259399,no,no,507,no
0.282271440738007,no,no,520,no
0.585435714379622,yes,yes,515,yes
0.529794960995109,no,yes,545,no
0.832959234636724,yes,yes,436,yes
0.136123508278338,yes,no,506,no
```

The following code loads this data and builds a classifier using the J48 decision tree, and then uses the model to predict if there will be a traffic jam today:

```
open WekaSharp.Classify
open WekaSharp.Dataset
open WekaSharp.Eval
open WekaSharp.Common
open weka
open weka.classifiers.trees

[<EntryPoint>]
let main argv =
    let traffic =
            @"C:\personal\raindata.txt"
            |> WekaSharp.Dataset.readCsv
            |> WekaSharp.Dataset.setClassIndexWithLastAttribute

    //Creating a decision tree classifier
    let classifier = WekaSharp.Classify.buildJ48 "J48 Decision Tree"
traffic

    //Printing the decision tree classifier.
    printfn "%A" classifier

    //Performing a classification
    let prediction = classifier.classifyInstance(traffic.instance(49))
```

```
//Printing the prediction
printfn "%A" prediction

//Printing the actual data instance
printfn "%A" (traffic.instance (49))

0
```

This produces the following output:

```
J48 pruned tree
------------------

rush_hour = no: no (51.0)
rush_hour = yes
|   rain_chance <= 0.773031: no (38.0/2.0)
|   rain_chance > 0.773031: yes (11.0)

Number of Leaves  :     3

Size of the tree :      5

1.0
0.884805,yes,yes,529,yes
```

The last two lines of this output are significant. They show that the program thinks that there could be a traffic build up, as "1" indicates the "yes" in the traffic column. You can be creative and add as many more features as you think contribute to the traffic jam build up. For example, you might want to consider if any construction work is underway on the road to home, if it rained yesterday, if it is a festive season, and so on.

The first part of the output shows the structure of the learnt decision tree model that has been used to predict the traffic jam.

Challenge yourself!

Now that you know how to use k-NN, logistic regression, and the J48 decision tree to predict classes, can you use whatever you learnt in this chapter to create an e-mail spam identification system? Solve it using all kinds of algorithms and then check your result.

Get the spam data from `http://archive.ics.uci.edu/ml/machine-learning-databases/spambase/`.

Summary

Congratulations on finishing yet another chapter. What you learned in this chapter is crucial for several complex machine learning activities. All the algorithms discussed in this chapter give a view of the underlying principals from several given examples (also called training sets). These types of algorithms are broadly classified under supervised learning.

You learnt how to use K-NN, a logistic regression model, and a J48 decision tree to predict the class/tag of an unknown entry.

In the next chapter, you will learn how to find similar products or items using several information retrieval metrics.

4
Information Retrieval

"Ways to find a needle in haystack"

Information overload is almost a passé term; however, it is still valid. Information retrieval is a big arena and most of it is far from being solved. However, that being said, we have come a long way and the results produced by some of the state-of-the-art information retrieval algorithms are really impressive. You may not know that you are using information retrieval but whenever you search for some documents on your PC or on the internet, you are actually using the product of an information retrieval algorithm in the background. So as the metaphor goes, finding the needle (read information/insight) in a haystack (read your data archive on your PC or on the web) is the key to successful business. This chapter is dedicated to showing you how you can code up some of the popular and useful information retrieval algorithms using F# and then use them in your problem domain.

Objective

After reading this chapter, you will be able to use several information retrieval algorithms, either as-is or in combination with other machine learning techniques to yield a better result. All the source code is available at `https://gist.github.com/sudipto80/5d91060e998ab383b274`.

Different IR algorithms you will learn

Information retrieval is sometimes referred to as IR. You will learn several algorithms in this chapter that are:

- **Distance based**: Two documents are matched based on their proximity, calculated by several distance metrics on the vector representation of the document

- **Set based**: Two documents are matched based on their proximity, calculated by several set based/fuzzy set based metrics based on the **bag of words** (**BoW**) model of the document

Don't worry if some of the phrases in this section don't make sense right now. By the end of this chapter, you will have a thorough understanding of these techniques and how to use them.

What interesting things can you do?

You will learn how the same algorithm can find similar cookies and identify the authors of digital documents from the words authors use. You will also learn how IR distance metrics can be used to group color images.

Information retrieval using tf-idf

Whenever you type some search term in your Windows search box, some documents appear matching your search term. There is a common, well-known, easy-to-implement algorithm that makes it possible to rank the documents based on the search term. Basically, the algorithm allows developers to assign some kind of score to each document in the result set. That score can be seen as a score of confidence that the system has on how much the user would like that result.

The score that this algorithm attaches with each document is a product of two different scores. The first one is called **term frequency** (**tf**) and the other one is called **inverse document frequency** (**idf**). Their product is referred to as **tf-idf** or "term frequency inverse document frequency".

Tf is the number of times a term occurs in a given document. Idf is the ratio between the total number of documents scanned and the number of documents in which a given search term is found. However, this ratio is not used as is. The log of this ration is used as idf, as shown next. The following is a term frequency and inverse term frequency example for the word "*example*":

$$tfidf\left("example", d_2\right) = tf\left("example", d_2\right) \times idf\left("example", D\right)$$

This is the same as:

$$tfidf\left("example", d_2\right) = 3 \times 0.3010 \approx 0.9030$$

Idf is normally calculated with the following formula:

$$\log \frac{N}{\left|\{d \in D : t \in d\}\right|}$$

The following is the code that demonstrates how to find the tf-idf score for the given search term; in this case, "*example*". Sentences are fabricated to match up the desired number of count of the word "example" in document 2; in this case, "sentence2". Here, D denotes the set of all the documents and d_2 denotes a second document:

```
let sentence1 = "this is a a sample"
let sentence2 = "this is another another example example example"

let word = "example"
let numberOfDocs = 2.

let tf1 = sentence1.Split ' ' |> Array.filter ( fun t -> t = word)
                              |> Array.length
let tf2 = sentence2.Split ' ' |> Array.filter ( fun t -> t = word)
                              |> Array.length

let docs = [|sentence1;sentence2|]
let foundIn = docs |> Array.map ( fun t -> t.Split ' '
                                          |> Array.filter ( fun z -> z = word))
                   |> Array.filter ( fun m -> m |> Array.length <> 0)
                   |> Array.length

let idf =  Operators.log10 ( numberOfDocs / float foundIn)
let pr1 = float  tf1 * idf
let pr2 = float tf2 * idf
printfn "%f %f" pr1 pr2
```

This produces the following output:

```
0.0  0.903090
```

This means that the second document is more closely related with the word "`example`" than the first one. In this case, this is one of the extreme cases where the word doesn't appear at all in one document and appears three times in the other. However, with the same word occurring multiple times in both the documents, you will get different scores for each document. You can think of these scores as the confidence scores for the association of the word and the document. The greater the score, the greater the confidence that the document has something related to that word.

Measures of similarity

In the following section, you will create a framework for finding several distance measures. A distance between two **probability distribution functions** (**pdf**) is an important way of knowing how close two entities are. One way to generate the pdfs from a histogram is to normalize the histogram.

Generating a PDF from a histogram

A histogram holds the number of times a value has occurred. For example, a text can be represented as a histogram where the histogram values represent the number of times a word appears in the text. For gray images, it can be the number of times each gray scale appears in the image.

In the following section, you will build a few modules that hold several distance metrics. The distance metric is a measure of how similar two objects are. It can also be called a measure of proximity.

The following metrics use the notation of P_i and Q_i to denote the ith value of either PDF. Let's say we have a histogram denoted by H, and there are N elements in the histogram. In this case, a rough estimate of P_i is $H(i)/N$. The following function does this transformation from histogram to pdf:

```
let toPdf (histogram:int list)=
        histogram |> List.map (fun t -> float t / float histogram.Length)
```

There are a couple of important assumptions made. First, we assume that the number of bins is equal to the number of elements. So the histogram and the pdf will have the same number of elements. That's not exactly correct in a mathematical sense. All the elements of a pdf should add up to 1. The following implementation of `histToPdf` guarantees that but it's not a good choice as it is not normalization. So resist the temptation to use this one:

```
let histToPdf (histogram:int list)=
        let sum = histogram |> List.sum
        histogram |> List.map (fun t -> float t / float sum)
```

Generating a histogram from a list of elements is simple. The function that takes a list and returns the histogram is as follows. F# has the function already built in; it is called **countBy**:

```
let listToHist (l : int list)=
        l |> List.countBy (fun t -> t)
```

Next is an example of how using these two functions, a list of integers can be transformed into a pdf. The following method takes a list of integers and returns the associated probability distribution:

```
let listToPdf (aList : int list)=
        aList |> List.countBy (fun t -> t)
              |> List.map snd
              |> toPdf
```

Here is how you can use it:

```
let list = [1;1;1;2;3;4;5;1;2]
let pdf = list |> listToPdf
```

I have captured the following in the F# interactive and got the following histogram from the preceding list:

```
val it : (int * int) list = [(1, 4); (2, 2); (3, 1); (4, 1); (5, 1)]
```

If you just project the second element of this histogram and store it in an `int` list, then you can represent the histogram in a list. So for this example, the histogram can be represented as:

```
let hist = [4;2;1;1;1]
```

Distance metrics are classified into several families based on their structural similarity. The following sections show how to work on these metrics using F# and use histograms as `int` list as input.

P and Q denote the vectors that represent the entity being compared. For example, for the document retrieval system, these numbers might indicate the number of times a given word occurred in each of the documents that are being compared. P_i denotes the ith element of the vector represented by P and Q_i denotes the ith element of the vector represented by Q. Some literature call these vectors the **profile vectors**.

Minkowski family

As you can see, when two pdfs are almost the same then this family of distance metrics tends to be zero, and when they are further apart, they lead to positive infinity. So if the distance metric between two pdfs is close to zero then we can conclude that they are similar and if the distance is more, then we can conclude otherwise. All the formulae of these metrics are special cases of what's known as **Minkowski** distance:

- **Euclidean distance**

$$d_{Euc} = \sqrt{\sum_{i=1}^{d} |P_i - Q_i|^2}$$

The following code implements Euclidean distance:

```
//Euclidean distance
let euclidean (p:int list)(q:int list) =
      List.zip p q |> List.sumBy (fun t -> float (fst t - snd t) ** 2.)
```

- **City block distance**

$$\sum_{i=1}^{d} |P_i - Q_i|$$

The following code implements City block distance:

```
//Cityblock distance
let cityBlock (p:int list)(q:int list) =
    List.zip (p|>toPdf) (q |> toPdf)
        |> List.map (fun t -> float (fst t  - snd t))
        |> List.sum
```

- **Chebyshev distance**

$$\max_{i} |P_i - Q_i|$$

The following code implements Chebyshev distance:

```
//Chebyshev distance
let chebyshev(p:int list)(q:int list) =
    List.zip (p|>toPdf) (q |> toPdf)
        |> List.map( fun t -> abs (fst t - snd t))
        |> List.max
```

L1 family

This family of distances relies on normalization to keep the values within a certain limit. All these metrics are of the form A/B where A is primarily a measure of proximity between the two pdfs P and Q. Most of the time A is calculated based on the absolute distance. For example, the numerator of the Sørensen distance is the City Block distance while the denominator is a normalization component that is obtained by adding each element of the two participating pdfs:

- **Sørensen**

$$d_{sor} = \frac{\sum_{i=1}^{d} |P_i - Q_i|}{\sum_{i=1}^{d} (P_i + Q_i)}$$

The following code implements Sørensen distance:

```
let sorensen  (p:int list)(q:int list) =
    let zipped = List.zip (p |> toPdf ) (q|>toPdf)
    let numerator = zipped  |> List.sumBy (fun t -> float (fst t - snd t))
    let denominator = zipped |> List.sumBy (fun t -> float (fst t + snd t))
    numerator / denominator
```

- **Gower distance**

$$d_{gow} = \frac{1}{d} \sum_{i=1}^{d} \frac{|P_i - Q_i|}{R_i}$$

$$= \frac{1}{d} \sum_{i=1}^{d} |P_i - Q_i|$$

The following code implements Gower distance. There could be division by zero if the collection `q` is empty:

```
let gower(p:int list)(q:int list)=
    //I love this. Free flowing fluid conversion
    //rather than cramping abs and fst t - snd t in a single line
    let numerator = List.zip (p|>toPdf) (q |> toPdf)|> List.map (fun t -> fst t - snd t)
                                |> List.map (fun z -> abs z)
                                |> List.map float
                                |> List.sum
                                |> float
    let denominator = float p.Length
    numerator / denominator
```

- **Soergel**

$$d_{sg} = \frac{\sum_{i=1}^{d} |P_i - Q_i|}{\sum_{i=1}^{d} \max(P_i, Q_i)}$$

The following code implements Soergel distance:

```
//Soergel Disance
let soergel (p:int list)(q:int list) =
    let zipped = List.zip (p|>toPdf) (q |> toPdf)
    let numerator =  zipped |> List.map(fun t -> abs( fst t - snd t))
                            |> List.sum
    let denominator = zipped |> List.map (fun t -> max (fst t ) (snd t))
                             |> List.sum
    float numerator / float denominator
```

- **kulczynski d**

$$d_{kul} = \frac{\sum_{i=1}^{d} |P_i - Q_i|}{\sum_{i=1}^{d} \min(P_i, Q_i)}$$

The following code implements Kulczynski d distance:

```
let kulczynski_d (p:int list)(q:int list) =
    let zipped = List.zip (p|>toPdf) (q |> toPdf)
    let numerator =  zipped |> List.map(fun t -> abs( fst t - snd t) )
                            |> List.sum
    let denominator = zipped |> List.map (fun t -> min (fst t ) (snd t))
                             |> List.sum
    float numerator / float denominator
```

- **kulczynski s**

  The following code implements Kulczynski s distance:

```
//kulczynski_s is the reciprocal of kulczynski_d distance
let kulczynski_s (p:int list)(q:int list) =
    1. / kulczynski_d p q
```

- **Canberra distance**

$$d_{Can} = \sum_{i=1}^{d} \frac{|P_i - Q_i|}{P_i + Q_i}$$

  The following code implements Canberra distance:

```
let canberra (p:int list)(q:int list) =
    let zipped = List.zip (p|>toPdf) (q |> toPdf)
    let numerator =  zipped |> List.map(fun t -> abs( fst t - snd t))
                            |> List.sum
    let denominator = zipped |> List.map (fun t ->fst t + snd t)
                             |> List.sum
    float numerator / float denominator
```

Intersection family

This family of distances tries to find the overlap between two participating pdfs:

- **Intersection**

$$s_{IS} = \sum_{i=1}^{d} \min(P_i, Q_i)$$

The following code implements Intersection distance:

```
let intersection(p:int list ) (q: int list) =
    List.zip (p|>toPdf) (q |> toPdf)
        |> List.map (fun t -> min (fst t) (snd t)) |> List.sum
```

- **Wave Hedges**

$$d_{WH} = \sum_{i=1}^{d} \left(1 - \frac{\min(P_i, Q_i)}{\max(P_i, Q_i)} \right)$$

The following code implements Wave Hedges distance:

```
let waveHedges (p:int list)(q:int list)=
    List.zip (p|>toPdf) (q |> toPdf)
        |> List.map ( fun t -> 1. - float( min (fst t) (snd t))
                                / float (max (fst t) (snd t)))
        |> List.sum
```

- **Czekanowski distance**

$$s_{Cze} = \frac{2\sum_{i=1}^{d} \min(P_i, Q_i)}{\sum_{i=1}^{d} (P_i + Q_i)}$$

The following code implements Czekanowski distance:

```
let czekanowski(p:int list)(q:int list) =
    let zipped  = List.zip (p|>toPdf) (q |> toPdf)
    let numerator = 2. * (zipped |> List.map (fun t -> min (fst t) (snd t))
                                 |> List.sum
                                 |> float)
    let denominator =  zipped |> List.map (fun t -> fst t + snd t) |> List.sum |> float
    numerator / denominator
```

- **Motyka**

$$s_{Mot} = \frac{\sum_{i=1}^{d} \min\left(P_i, Q_i\right)}{\sum_{i=1}^{d} \left(P_i + Q_i\right)}$$

The following code implements Motyka distance:

```
let motyka(p:int list)(q:int list)=
    let zipped = List.zip (p|>toPdf) (q |> toPdf)
    let numerator = zipped |> List.map (fun t -> min (fst t) (snd t))
                           |> List.sum |> float
    let denominator = zipped |> List.map (fun t -> fst t + snd t)
                             |> List.sum |> float
    numerator / denominator
```

- **Ruzicka**

$$s_{Ruz} = \frac{\sum_{i=1}^{d} \min\left(P_i, Q_i\right)}{\sum_{i=1}^{d} \max\left(P_i, Q_i\right)}$$

The following code implements Ruzicka distance:

```
let ruzicka (p:int list) (q:int list) =
    let zipped = List.zip (p|>toPdf) (q |> toPdf)
    let numerator = zipped |> List.map (fun t -> min (fst t) (snd t))
                           |> List.sum |> float
    let denominator = zipped |> List.map (fun t -> max (fst t) (snd t))
                             |> List.sum |> float
    numerator / denominator
```

Inner Product family

Distances belonging to this family are calculated by some product of pairwise elements from both the participating pdfs. Then this product is normalized with a value also calculated from the pairwise elements:

- **Inner Product**

$$s_{IP} = P \bullet Q = \sum_{j=1}^{d} P_i Q_i$$

The following code implements Inner Product distance:

```
let innerProduct(p:int list)(q:int list)=
    List.zip (p|>toPdf) (q |> toPdf)
        |> List.sumBy (fun t -> fst t * snd t)
```

- **Harmonic mean**

$$s_{HM} = 2\sum_{i=1}^{d} \frac{P_i Q_i}{P_i + Q_i}$$

The following code implements Harmonic distance:

```
let harmonicMean(p:int list)(q:int list)=
   2. * (List.zip (p|>toPdf) (q |> toPdf)
      |> List.sumBy (fun t -> ( fst t * snd t )/
                              (fst t + snd t)))
```

- **Cosine similarity**

$$s_{Cos} = \frac{\sum_{i=1}^{d} P_i Q_i}{\sqrt{\sum_{i=1}^{d} P_i^2}\sqrt{\sum_{i=1}^{d} Q_i^2}}$$

The following code implements Cosine similarity distance:

```
let cosineSimilarity(p:int list)(q:int list)=
    let zipped = List.zip p  q //(p|>toPdf) (q |> toPdf)
    let prod  (x,y) = float x *  float y
    let numerator = zipped |> List.map prod |> List.sum
    let denominator  =  sqrt ( p|> List.map sqr |> List.sum |> float) *
                        sqrt ( q|> List.map sqr |> List.sum |> float)
    numerator / denominator
```

- **Kumar Hassebrook**

$$S_{Jac} = \frac{\sum_{i=1}^{d} P_i Q_i}{\sum_{i=1}^{d} P_i^2 + \sum_{i=1}^{d} Q_i^2 - \sum_{i=1}^{d} P_i Q_i}$$

The following code implements Kumar Hassebrook distance:

```
let kumarHassebrook (p:int list) (q:int list) =
    let sqr x = x * x
    let zipped = List.zip (p|>toPdf) (q |> toPdf)
    let numerator = zipped |> List.map (fun t -> fst t * snd t )
                           |> List.sum |> float
    let denominator =  (p |> List.map sqr |> List.sum |> float ) +
                       (q |> List.map sqr |> List.sum |> float ) - numerator

    numerator / denominator
```

- **Dice coefficient**

$$S_{Dice} = \frac{2\sum_{i=1}^{d} P_i Q_i}{\sum_{i=1}^{d} P_i^2 + \sum_{i=1}^{d} Q_i^2}$$

The following code implements Dice coefficient:

```
let dicePoint(p:int list)(q:int list)=
    let zipped = List.zip (p|>toPdf) (q |> toPdf)
    let numerator = zipped |> List.map (fun t -> fst t * snd t)
                           |> List.sum
                           |> float
    let denominator  =  (p |> List.map sqr |> List.sum |> float)  +
                        (q |> List.map sqr |> List.sum |> float)

    numerator / denominator
```

Fidelity family or squared-chord family

This family of distances uses a square root as an instrument to keep the distance within a certain limit. Sometimes other functions, such as log, are also used:

- **Fidelity**

$$s_{Fid} = \sum_{i=1}^{d} \sqrt{P_i Q_i}$$

The following code implements Fidelity distance:

```
let fidelity(p:int list)(q:int list)=
    List.zip (p|>toPdf) (q |> toPdf)
        |> List.map  (fun t -> float (fst t) * float (snd t))
        |> List.map sqrt
        |> List.sum
```

- **Bhattacharya**

$$d_B = -\ln \sum_{i=1}^{d} \sqrt{P_i Q_i}$$

The following code implements Bhattacharya distance:

```
let bhattacharya(p:int list)(q:int list)=
    -log (fidelity p q)
```

- **Hellinger**

$$d_H = 2\sqrt{1 - \sum_{i=1}^{d} \sqrt{P_i Q_i}}$$

The following code implements Hellinger distance:

```
let hellinger(p:int list)(q:int list)=
    let prod (a,b) = float a * float b
    let product = List.zip (p|>toPdf) (q |> toPdf)
                        |> List.map prod
                        |> List.map sqrt
                        |> List.sum
```

- **Matusita**

$$d_M = \sqrt{2 - 2\sum_{i=1}^{d} \sqrt{P_i Q_i}\ )}$$

The following code implements Matusita distance:

```
let matusita(p:int list)(q:int list)=
    let prod (a,b) = float a * float b
    let value =2. - 2. *
                ( List.zip (p|>toPdf) (q |> toPdf)
                        |> List.map prod
                        |> List.map sqrt
                        |> List.sum)
    value |> abs |> sqrt
```

- **Squared Chord**

$$d_{sqc} = \sum_{i=1}^{d} \left(\sqrt{P_i} - \sqrt{Q_i}\right)^2$$

The following code implements Squared Chord distance:

```
let squarredChord(p:int list)(q:int list)=
    List.zip (p|>toPdf) (q |> toPdf)
        |> List.map (fun t -> sqrt (fst t ) - sqrt (snd t))
        |> List.sum
```

Squared L2 family

This is almost the same as the L1 family, except that it got rid of the expensive square root operation and relies on squares instead. However, that should not be an issue. Sometimes the squares can be quite large so a normalization scheme is provided by dividing the result of the squared sum by another squared sum, as done in "Divergence".

- **Squared Euclidean**

$$d_{sqe} = \sum_{i=1}^{d} (P_i - Q_i)^2$$

The following code implements Squared Euclidean distance. For most purpose this can be used instead of Euclidean distance as it is computationally cheap and performs just as well:

```
let squaredEuclidean (p:int list)(q:int list)=
   let toSquare x = x * x
   List.zip (p|>toPdf) (q |> toPdf)
       |> List.sumBy (fun t-> (fst t - snd t) ** 2.0)
```

- **Squared Chi**

$$d_{SqChi} = \sum_{i=1}^{d} \frac{(P_i - Q_i)^2}{P_i + Q_i}$$

The following code implements Squared Chi distance:

```
let squaredChi(p:int list)(q:int list)=
    List.zip (p|>toPdf) (q |> toPdf)
       |> List.map (fun t -> (fst t - snd t ) ** 2.0 / (fst t + snd t))
       |> List.sum
```

- **Pearson's Chi**

$$d_P(P,Q)=\sum_{i=1}^{d}\frac{(P_i-Q_i)^2}{Q_i}$$

The following code implements Pearson's Chi distance:

```
let pearsonsChi(p:int list)(q:int list)=
    List.zip (p|>toPdf) (q |> toPdf)
        |> List.map (fun t -> (fst t - snd t ) ** 2.0 / snd t)
        |> List.sum
```

- **Neyman's Chi**

$$d_N(P,Q)=\sum_{i=1}^{d}\frac{(P_i-Q_i)^2}{P_i}$$

The following code implements Neyman's Chi distance:

```
let neymanChi(p:int list)(q:int list)=
    List.zip (p|>toPdf) (q |> toPdf)
        |> List.map (fun t -> (fst t - snd t ) ** 2.0 / fst t)
        |> List.sum
```

- **Probabilistic Symmetric Chi**

$$d_{PChii}=2\sum_{i=1}^{d}\frac{(P_i-Q_i)^2}{P_i+Q_i}$$

The following code implements Probabilistic Symmetric Chi distance:

```
let probabilisticSymmetricChi(p:int list)(q:int list)=
   2.0 * squaredChi p q
```

- **Divergence**

$$d_{Div} = 2\sum_{i=1}^{d} \frac{(P_i - Q_i)^2}{(P_i + Q_i)^2}$$

The following code implements Divergence distance. This metric is useful when the elements of the collections have elements in different orders of magnitude. This normalization will make the distance properly adjusted for several kinds of usage:

```
let divergence(p:int list)(q:int list)=
    List.zip (p|>toPdf) (q |> toPdf)
        |> List.map (fun t -> (fst t - snd t) ** 2. / (fst t + snd t) ** 2.)
        |> List.sum
```

- **Clark**

$$d_{Clk} = \sqrt{\sum_{i=1}^{d} \left(\frac{|P_i + Q_i|}{P_i + Q_i} \right)^2}$$

The following code implements Clark's distance:

```
let clark(p:int list)(q:int list)=

    sqrt( List.zip (p|>toPdf) (q |> toPdf)
    |> List.map (fun t ->  float( abs( fst t - snd t))
                          / (float (fst t + snd t)))

    |> List.map (fun t -> t * t)
    |> List.sum )
```

- **Additive Symmetric Chi**

$$d_{AdChi} = \sum_{i=1}^{b} \frac{(P_i - Q_i)^2 (P_i + Q_i)}{P_i Q_i}$$

The following code implements Additive Symmetric Chi distance:

```
let additiveSymmetricChi(p:int list)(q:int list)=
    List.zip (p|>toPdf) (q |> toPdf)
        |> List.map (fun t -> (fst t - snd t ) ** 2. * (fst t + snd t) / (fst t * snd t))
        |> List.sum
```

Shannon's Entropy family

This family of distances can probably be declared as "one-over-another" family also, because it uses the ratio of pairwise items from pdfs to determine the following:

- **Kulback Leibler**

$$d_{KL} = \sum_{i=1}^{d} P_i \ln \frac{P_i}{Q_i}$$

The following code implements Kulback Leibler's distance:

```
let kullbackLeibler(p:int list)(q:int list)=
    List.zip (p|>toPdf) (q |> toPdf)
        |> List.map (fun t -> float( fst t) * log (float (fst t )/float (snd t)))
        |> List.sum
```

- **Jeffrey's**

$$d_J = \sum_{i=1}^{d} (P_i - Q_i) \ln \frac{P_i}{Q_i}$$

The following code implements Jeffrey distance:

```
let jeffreys(p:int list)(q:int list)=
    List.zip (p|>toPdf) (q |> toPdf)
        |> List.map (fun t -> float( fst t - snd t) * log (float (fst t )/float (snd t)))
        |> List.sum
```

- **K Divergence**

$$d_{Kdiv} = \sum_{i=1}^{d} P_i \ln \frac{2P_i}{P_i + Q_i}$$

The following code implements K Divergence distance:

```
let k_Divergence(p:int list)(q:int list)=
    List.zip (p|>toPdf) (q |> toPdf)
        |> List.map (fun t -> fst t * log (2.0 *  fst t) / (fst t + snd t))
        |> List.sum
```

- **Topose**

$$d_{Top} = \sum_{i=1}^{d} \left(P_i \ln\left(\frac{2P_i}{P_i + Q_i} \right) + Q_i \ln\left(\frac{2Q_i}{P_i + Q_i} \right) \right)$$

The following code implements Topose distance:

```
let topose (p:int list)(q:int list) =
    let sum ( a , b ) = a + b
    //Higher order functions in action!
    let firstByBoth ( a , b) = float a / float (sum (a , b))
    let secondByBoth ( a , b)= float b / float (sum (a , b))
    let zipped = List.zip (p|> List.map (fun t -> float t  / float p.Length))
                          (q|> List.map (fun t -> float t  / float p.Length))
    zipped |> List.map ( fun t -> float (fst t) * firstByBoth t + float (snd t) * secondByBoth t)
           |> List.sum
```

- **Jensen Shanon**

$$d_{JS} = \frac{1}{2} \left[\sum_{i=1}^{d} P_i \ln\left(\frac{2P_i}{P_i + Q_i} \right) + \sum_{i=1}^{d} Q_i \ln\left(\frac{2Q_i}{P_i + Q_i} \right) \right]$$

[Note that the Jensen Shanon metric is half of the Topose distance. So calculating that becomes simple.]

The following code implements Jensen Shanon distance:

```
let jensenShanon(p:int list)(q:int list)=
    0.5 * topose p q
```

- **Jensen Difference**

$$d_{JD} = \sum_{i=1}^{b} \left[\frac{P_i \ln P_i + Q_i \ln Q_i}{2} - \left(\frac{P_i + Q_i}{2} \right) \ln \left(\frac{P_i + Q_i}{2} \right) \right]$$

The following code implements Jensen Difference:

```
let jensenDifference (p:int list) (q:int list) =
    let zipped = List.zip (p|>toPdf) (q |> toPdf)
    let left = zipped |> List.map (fun t -> fst t * log (fst t) + snd t * log (snd t))
                      |> List.map (fun t -> t / 2.)
    let right = zipped |> List.map (fun t -> ((fst t  + snd t) * 0.5 ) * log (0.5*(fst t + snd t)))

    List.zip left right |> List.map (fun t -> fst t - snd t) |> List.sum
```

Combinations

These metrics are an attempt to bring the best of several other distance metrics together and can be effective with noisy data:

- **Taneja**

$$d_{TJ} = \sum_{i=1}^{d} \left(\frac{P_i + Q_i}{2} \right) \ln \left(\frac{P_i + Q_i}{2\sqrt{P_i Q_i}} \right)$$

The following code implements Taneja distance:

```
let taneja(p:int list)(q:int list)=
    List.zip (p|>toPdf) (q |> toPdf)
       |> List.map ( fun t ->
          float(fst t  + snd t )/2.0
            * log ( float ( fst t + snd t)/ 2. * sqrt (fst t * snd t)))
       |> List.sum
```

- **Kumar Johnson**

$$d_{KJ} = \sum_{i=1}^{d} \left(\frac{\left(P_i^2 - Q_i^2\right)^2}{2\left(PiQi\right)^{3/2}} \right)$$

The following code implements Kumar Johnson distance:

```
let kumarJohnson(p:int list)(q:int list)=
    List.zip (p|>toPdf) (q |> toPdf)
       |> List.map (fun t -> (fst t ** 2. - snd t ** 2.) ** 2.
                          / (2. * (fst t * snd t) ** 1.5))
       |> List.sum
```

Set-based similarity measures

To check how close two sets are, you can use these metrics. These metrics are used internally in several algorithms for finding similar sets. For example, in collaborative filtering, these set-based proximity measures can be used to find users whose preferences match up better than others:

- **Jaccard index**

$$J(A,B) = \frac{|A \cap B|}{|A \cup B|} = \frac{|A \cap B|}{|A| + |B| - |A \cap B|}$$

The following code implements Jaccard index:

```
let jaccard (first : string list) (second:string list) =
    let setOfFirst = first |> Set.ofList
    let setOfSecond  = second |> Set.ofList
    match first.Length + second.Length with
       | 0 -> 0.0 //If the union is zero there can't be any match
                  //But in set theory two empty sets are considered equal
                  //So we can return 0.0 to
       | _ -> float  (Set.intersect setOfFirst setOfSecond).Count /
              float  (Set.union setOfFirst setOfSecond).Count
```

- **Tversky index**

$$S(X,Y)=\frac{|X\cap Y|}{|X\cap Y|+\alpha|X-Y|+\beta|Y-X|}$$

The following code implements Tversky index:

```
//A generic tversky index function
let tverskyIndexG (first :'a list)(second : 'a list) =
    let X = Set.ofList first
    let Y = Set.ofList second
    let alpha  = 0.34
    let beta  = 0.42
    let I  = Set.intersect X Y |> Set.count
    let Diff = X -  Y |> Set.count
    let Diff2 = Y - X |> Set.count

    float I / float (I + Diff + Diff2)
```

Similarity of asymmetric binary attributes

Let two objects, s and t, be described by two binary vectors, x and y; each comprised p variables with values 0/1. The binary similarity measures are commonly calculated from the data reported in Table 1, where a, b, c, and d are the frequencies of the events (**x = 1** and **y = 1**), (**x = 1** and **y = 0**), (**x = 0** and **y = 1**), and (**x = 0** and **y = 0**) respectively, in the pair of binary vectors describing the objects s and t; p is the total number of variables, equal to a +b + c + d, which is the length of each binary vector.

	$y=1$		
$x=1$	a	b	
$x=0$	c	d	
		$b+d$	p

Table 1—Frequency table of the four possible combinations of two binary variables

In other words,

- **a** is the number of variables equal to one for both objects (common "presences")
- **d** is the number of variables equal to zero for both objects (common "absences")
- **a + b** is the number of variables equal to one for the s-th object
- **a + c** is the number of variables equal to one for the t-th object

The following method finds a, b, c, and d given two sets. For simplicity, I have used couple of string lists to represent the two sets. This approach is correct without any loss of generality:

```
let private getABCD (first :string list)(second : string list) =
    let all = Set.union (first |> Set.ofList) (second |> Set.ofList) |> Set.toList
    let firstMatches = all |> List.map (fun t -> first |> List.contains t )
    let secondMatches = all |> List.map (fun t ->  second |> List.contains t )
    let zipped = List.zip firstMatches secondMatches
    let A = zipped |> List.filter (fun t -> fst t = true && snd t = true) |> List.length
    let B = zipped |> List.filter (fun t -> fst t = false && snd t = true) |> List.length
    let C = zipped |> List.filter (fun t -> fst t = true && snd t = false) |> List.length
    let D = zipped |> List.filter (fun t -> fst t = false && snd t = false) |> List.length
    [|A ; B ; C ;D|] |> Array.map float
```

The following is a list of some prominent asymmetric similarity measures:

- **Sokal - Sneath 1 (1963)**

$$s_{SS1} = \frac{a}{a+2b+c}$$

The following code implements Sokal-Sneath 1 index:

```
let SS1 (first :string list)(second : string list) =
    let abcd = getABCD first second
    let a = abcd.[0]
    let b = abcd.[1]
    let c = abcd.[2]
    let d = abcd.[3]
    a / ( a + 2. * b + 2. * c)
```

- **Sokal - Sneath 2 (1963)**

$$s_{SS2} = \frac{2a+2d}{p+a+d}$$

The following code implements Sokal-Sneath 2 index:

```
let SS2 (first :string list)(second : string list) =
    let abcd = getABCD first second
    let a = abcd.[0]
    let b = abcd.[1]
    let c = abcd.[2]
    let d = abcd.[3]
    (2. * a + 2. * d )/ (float first.Length + a + d)
```

- **Sokal - Sneath 3(1963)**

$$s_{SS3} = \frac{1}{4} \cdot \left[\frac{a}{a+b} + \frac{a}{a+c} + \frac{d}{b+d} + \frac{d}{c+d} \right]$$

The following code implements Sokal-Sneath 3 index:

```
let SS3 (first :string list)(second : string list) =
    let abcd = getABCD first second
    let a = abcd.[0]
    let b = abcd.[1]
    let c = abcd.[2]
    let d = abcd.[3]
    0.25 * ( a / (a + b) + a / (a + c) + d / (b + d) + d / (c + d))
```

- **Sokal - Sneath 4 (1963)**

$$s_{SS4} = \frac{a}{\sqrt{(a+b)(a+c)}} \cdot \frac{d}{\sqrt{(b+d)(c+d)}}$$

The following code implements Sokal-Sneath 4 index:

```
let SS4 (first :string list)(second : string list) =
    let abcd = getABCD first second
    let a = abcd.[0]
    let b = abcd.[1]
    let c = abcd.[2]
    let d = abcd.[3]
    (a / (sqrt ((a + b) * (a + c))) ) *
    (d / (sqrt ((b + d) * (c + d))) )
```

- **Jaccard coefficient**

  The following code implements Jaccard coefficient:

```
//For calculating similarity between asymteric binary attributes
let jaccardCoeff (first : string list) ( second : string list ) =
    let all = Set.union (first |> Set.ofList) (second |> Set.ofList) |> Set.toList
    let firstMatches = all |> List.map (fun t -> first |> List.contains t )
    let secondMatches = all |> List.map (fun t ->  second |> List.contains t )
    let zipped = List.zip firstMatches secondMatches
    let M11 = zipped |> List.filter (fun t -> fst t = true && snd t = true) |> List.length
    let M01 = zipped |> List.filter (fun t -> fst t = false && snd t = true) |> List.length
    let M10 = zipped |> List.filter (fun t -> fst t = true && snd t = false) |> List.length
    let M00 = zipped |> List.filter (fun t -> fst t = false && snd t = false) |> List.length
    let J = float M11 / float (M01 + M10 + M11)
    J//return the Jaccard coefficient
```

- **Simple matching coefficient**

$$SMC = \frac{\textit{Number of Matching Attributes}}{\textit{Number of Attributes}} = \frac{M_{00} + M_{11}}{M_{00} + M_{01} + M_{10} + M_{11}}$$

These are described as follows:

  - M_{11} represents the total number of attributes where A and B both have a value of 1
  - M_{01} represents the total number of attributes where the attribute of A is 0 and the attribute of B is 1
  - M_{10} represents the total number of attributes where the attribute of A is 1 and the attribute of B is 0
  - M_{00} represents the total number of attributes where A and B both have a value of 0

The following code implements Simple matching coefficient:

```
let simpleMatchingCoeff  (first : string list) ( second : string list )=
    let all = Set.union (first |> Set.ofList) (second |> Set.ofList) |> Set.toList
    let firstMatches = all |> List.map (fun t -> first |> List.contains t )
    let secondMatches = all |> List.map (fun t ->  second |> List.contains t )
    let zipped = List.zip firstMatches secondMatches
    let M11 = zipped |> List.filter (fun t -> fst t = true && snd t = true) |> List.length
    let M01 = zipped |> List.filter (fun t -> fst t = false && snd t = true) |> List.length
    let M10 = zipped |> List.filter (fun t -> fst t = true && snd t = false) |> List.length
    let M00 = zipped |> List.filter (fun t -> fst t = false && snd t = false) |> List.length

    let numerator = M11 + M00
    let denominator  = M10 + M01 - M11 + M00

    float numerator / float denominator
```

- **Tanimoto coefficient**
  - *Nc* represents the total number of attributes where A and B both have a value of 1
  - *Na* represents the total number of attributes where the attribute of A is 1
  - *Nb* represents the total number of attributes where the attribute of B is 1

The following code implements Tanimoto coefficient:

```
let tanimotoCoeff (first : string list) ( second : string list ) =
    let all = Set.union (first |> Set.ofList) (second |> Set.ofList) |> Set.toList
    let firstMatches = all |> List.map (fun t -> first |> List.contains t )
    let secondMatches = all |> List.map (fun t ->  second |> List.contains t )
    let zipped = List.zip firstMatches secondMatches
    let Nc = zipped |> List.filter (fun t -> fst t = true && snd t = true) |> List.length
    let Na = firstMatches |> List.filter (fun t -> t = true) |> List.length
    let Nb = secondMatches |> List.filter (fun t -> t = true) |> List.length
    float Nc / float (Na + Nb - Nc)
```

Some example usages of distance metrics

Here are some example usages of the distance metrics defined earlier.

Finding similar cookies using asymmetric binary similarity measures

You might be thinking, well I have all these several distance/proximity metrics but how can I use them in my application?

Here is the simple answer to that. Every problem domain can be represented by entities and every entity can be represented by a vector. This vector is sometimes referred to as profile vector. For example, let's say you want to find out the author of a digital document. If you have a sample of 10 such authors then you have 10 different profile vectors. Now when you get a new entry, you can find the closest match by transforming your profile vectors (which can be histograms of words the author uses) to pdfs and then applying any of the similarity measures.

So the key is to identify and realize that every information retrieval problem essentially boils down to a vector/pdf proximity problem. Let's say you are trying to find similar biscuits. This can be modeled as an asymmetric similarity problem. Because every biscuit will have different ingredients and the intersection of ingredients can be very sparse, if you represent each biscuit by a profile vector and then use the Simple matching coefficient or any of the Sokal Sneath coefficients, you should be able to tell the degree to which two biscuits are similar.

The following variables store the ingredients of four different biscuits. The task is to identify biscuits that are similar to each other:

```
let biscuitA = ["refined wheat flour";"sugar";"edible vegetable oil";
                 "edible coconut products";"invert syrup";"milk solids";
                 "edible starch";"raising agent";"edible common salt";
                 "baking powder";"solbake";"emulsifier"]

let biscuitB = ["refined wheat flour";"cocoa powder";"suger";"cocoa butter";
                 "dextrose";"lecithin";"vanillin";"edible vegetable oil";
                 "raising agent";"cocoa solids";"edible common salt";"emulsifier"]

let biscuitC = ["refined wheat flour";"suger";"cocoa solids";
                 "cocoa butter";"dextrose";"emulsifier";
                "edible vegitable fat";"desiccated coconut butter";
                "skimmed milk powder";"raising agents";"vanillin"]

let biscuitD = ["refined wheat flour";"suger";"edible vegitable oil";
                 "edible starch";"arrowroot";"maize";
                 "invert syrup";"milk solids";"raising agents";
                 "dough conditioner";"edible common salt";"emulsifier"]
```

The following lines find similarity between biscuit A and the other biscuits, and biscuit B and the other biscuits by using some of the measures described earlier. Pause for a while and scan the ingredient lists yourself. You will find that the ingredient list of biscuit A is similar to that of biscuit D and that's an indication that these two biscuits are similar. On the other hand, biscuit B and biscuit C have very similar ingredient lists. This means that biscuit B and biscuit C are similar.

```
//Finding similarities between Biscuit B and other biscuits
//using tanimoto coefficient
let simBC_t = tanimotoCoeff biscuitB biscuitC
let simBD_t = tanimotoCoeff biscuitB biscuitD
let simBA_t = tanimotoCoeff biscuitB biscuitA

//Finding similarities between Biscuit A and other biscuits
//using tanimoto coefficient
let simAB_t = tanimotoCoeff biscuitA biscuitB
let simAC_t = tanimotoCoeff biscuitA biscuitC
let simAD_t = tanimotoCoeff biscuitA biscuitD

//Finding similarities between Biscuit B and other biscuits
//using simple matching coefficient
let simBC_s = simpleMatchingCoeff biscuitB biscuitC
let simBD_s = simpleMatchingCoeff biscuitB biscuitD
let simBA_s = simpleMatchingCoeff biscuitB biscuitA
```

```
//Finding similarities between Biscuit A and other biscuits
//using simple matching coefficient
let simAB_s = simpleMatchingCoeff biscuitA biscuitB
let simAC_s = simpleMatchingCoeff biscuitA biscuitC
let simAD_s = simpleMatchingCoeff biscuitA biscuitD

//Finding similarities between Biscuit B and other biscuits
//using sokal sneath 1  coefficient
let simBC_ss = SS1 biscuitB biscuitC
let simBD_ss = SS1 biscuitB biscuitD
let simBA_ss = SS1 biscuitB biscuitA

//Finding similarities between Biscuit A and other biscuits
//using sokal sneath 1  coefficient
let simAB_ss = SS1 biscuitA biscuitB
let simAC_ss = SS1 biscuitA biscuitC
let simAD_ss = SS1 biscuitA biscuitD
```

From these results you can see that it is proved that biscuit A and biscuit D are similar, and biscuit B and biscuit C are similar.

Grouping/clustering color images based on Canberra distance

Color images can be grouped together by calculating the distance between their histogram of colors:

- Image 1:

- Image 2:

For example, the following code finds the similarities between the rose and the potato images:

```
open System.IO
let image = System.Drawing.Image.FromFile(@"C:\personal\rose.jpg")
let image2  = System.Drawing.Image.FromFile(@"C:\personal\potato.jpg")

let ms = new MemoryStream()
image.Save(ms,System.Drawing.Imaging.ImageFormat.Jpeg)
let bytes = ms.ToArray() |> Array.map int |> List.ofArray

let ms2 = new MemoryStream()
image2.Save(ms2,System.Drawing.Imaging.ImageFormat.Jpeg)
let bytes2 = ms2.ToArray() |> Array.map int |> List.ofArray

let bytesPDF = listToHist bytes |> List.map snd
let bytesPDF2   = listToHist bytes2 |> List.map snd

let simCanberra = canberra bytesPDF bytesPDF2
```

This code produces the following output:

```
val simCanberra : float = 0.1598777115
```

This means that there is only a 15% chance that the two images are similar. If two images are exactly the same, then Canberra distance will be zero.

This means we can group together similar images by finding the distance between their color histograms. I have selected these images randomly. You can use your own images and the results would be similar.

Summary

Congratulations on finishing yet another chapter. In this chapter, you learned how different similarity measures work and when to use which one to find the closest match. Edmund Burke said that, "It's the nature of every greatness not to be exact", and I can't agree more. Most of the time, users aren't really sure what they are looking for. So providing a binary answer of yes or no, or found or not found is not that useful. Striking the middle ground by attaching a confidence score to each result is the key. Techniques that you learned in this chapter will prove to be useful when we deal with recommender system and anomaly detection, because both these fields rely heavily on the IR techniques. The IR techniques are successfully applied to document clustering, digital author identification, color image and video clustering, and content-based recommender systems, to name a few.

5
Collaborative Filtering

"People who bought this also bought these."

When you shop online, the site recommends some items to you based on your shopping history and the products that you looked at and probably liked. The system that generates these recommendations is known as a recommendation engine. There are several types of state-of-the-art algorithms used to create a recommendation engine. In this chapter, a couple of such types of algorithms will be discussed, namely "collaborative filtering" and "content-based filtering".

Objective

After reading this chapter, you will be able to understand how some of the sites recommend items based on what products you have rated and based on your item browsing history. You will understand the mathematics behind collaborative filtering and how these can be applied to your problem domain.

Different classification algorithms you will learn

The following algorithms will be discussed at length:

- General non-personalized recommendations for a category of items
- User-user collaborative filtering
- User-user collaborative filtering with variations on similarity measures
- Item-item collaborative filtering
- Item-item collaborative filtering with variations

You will also learn how to evaluate recommendation engines using several evaluation metrics for different purposes, such as prediction accuracy, ranking accuracy in the context of top-N recommendations, and so on.

Vocabulary of collaborative filtering

The design of collaborative filters is influenced by two factors, which are as follows:

- **Users** (the people for whom the recommendation is being provided)
- **Items** (the products for which the recommendation is being provided)

Based on these two entities, there are two major varieties of collaborative filtering methods. The first of these methods takes the similarity between users to recommend items. This is known as **User-User collaborative filtering** or **User k-Nearest Neighbors**.

If the number of users of a recommender system is denoted by m and the number of items is denoted by n and if $m >> n$ (m is much greater than n) then user-user collaborative filtering suffers from performance hiccups. In this case, item-item collaborative filtering (which relies on the similarity of the items) is often implemented.

In the next few sections, these two algorithms will be discussed at length.

Baseline predictors

Before delving into true collaborative filtering, let's look at some baseline predictors that can predict ratings for new users who haven't rated anything yet, which makes it almost impossible to find out the neighborhood of such users. For such users, a basic baseline rating can be the average of all ratings. The problem with applying collaborative filtering in order to predict the ratings of items for new users is referred to as **Cold Start** in collaborative filtering literature.

The baseline predictor is normally denoted by $b_{u,i}$ for user u and item i. The base case where the baseline is set as equal to the global average of all ratings is given by the following formula:

$$b_{u,i} = \mu$$

However, this can be optimized using the average of that user's rating for other items (if any are available) or the average rating for that particular item (given by all other users). In these two cases, the baseline predictor is calculated using the following formulae:

$$b_{u,i} = \bar{r}_u$$

$$b_{u,i} = \bar{r}_i$$

Note that the subscript u is used to denote the user and the subscript i is used to denote the item. This notation is pretty standard across all collaborative filtering literature.

The baseline can be further enhanced by combining the user mean with the average deviation from the user mean rating for a given item. Generally, a baseline predictor of the following form is used:

$$b_{u,i} = \mu + b_u + b_i$$

b_u and b_i are the user and item baseline predictors, respectively. These are defined by the following formulae:

$$b_u = \frac{1}{|I_u|} \sum_{i \in I_u} (r_{u,i} - \mu)$$

$$b_i = \frac{1}{|U_i|} \sum_{u \in U_i} (r_{u,i} - b_u - \mu)$$

The following function returns the baseline predictor as discussed:

```
//Non personalized baseline predictor
let baseline (ratings:(float list)list) =
    let mu = ratings |> List.map ( fun ra -> [for i in 0 .. ra.Length - 1 -> ra.[i]]
                                          |> List.filter (fun t -> t <> 0.0)
                                          |> List.average)
                     |> List.average
    let mutable bu = ratings |> List.sumBy (fun rating -> [for i in 0 .. rating.Length - 1 -> rating.[i]]
                                                        |> List.filter (fun ri -> ri <> 0.0)
                                                        |> List.sumBy (fun ri -> ri - mu))

    bu <- bu / float ratings.[0].Length
    let mutable bi = ratings |> List.sumBy (fun ra -> [for i in 0 .. ra.Length - 1 -> ra.[i]]
                                                    |> List.filter (fun t -> t <> 0.0)
                                                    |> List.sumBy (fun z -> z - bu - mu))

    bi <- bi / float ratings.Length
    mu + bu + bi
```

You can get the source code from `https://gist.github.com/sudipto80/d257f8da8ed32b16fec3`

Basis of User-User collaborative filtering

As the name suggests, collaborative filtering is filtering with the help of others in a collaborative environment. The main idea is that users with the same product preferences provide similar ratings to similar products. So, if two users are quite similar in terms of their taste in movies, then they will probably rate a movie in the same manner. Either they both will love it or both will hate it.

The list of similar users is known as the neighborhood of the user for whom the recommendations are being calculated. The neighborhood is calculated based on some kind of a distance metric. First, the distance metric is calculated for all users (with users for whom the recommendation is being calculated). Then the users are sorted in ascending order of this metric value and the top-N users (N has to be determined by the design) are chosen to represent the neighborhood.

The most commonly used distance metric is **Pearson's correlation coefficient**. This metric is calculated with the following formula for two collections x and y of the same length:

$$r = \frac{\sum_i (x_i - \bar{x})(y_i - \bar{y})}{\sqrt{\sum_i (x_i - \bar{x})^2} \sqrt{\sum_i (y_i - \bar{y})^2}}$$

Here, $\overline{x}$ (read: the $\overline{x}$ bar) represents the average of the numbers in the collection $\overline{x}$ and $\overline{y}$ (read: the $\overline{y}$ bar) represents the average of the numbers in the collection $\overline{y}$. x_i represents the *i*th element of the collection $\overline{x}$ and y_i represent the ith element of the collection $\overline{y}$. Here is an example of Pearson's correlation coefficient calculated for a couple of arrays in F#:

```
let x = [1.;2.;3.;4.;5.]
let y = [1.;2.;2.;3.;4.]
let z = [3;4]

let x_bar = List.average x
let y_bar = List.average y

let numerator =
    List.zip x y
    |> List.sumBy (fun item -> (fst item - x_bar)*(snd item - y_bar))

let d1 = x |> List.sumBy(fun xi -> (xi - x_bar) ** 2.0)
let d2 = y |> List.sumBy(fun yi -> (yi - y_bar) ** 2.0)

let denominator = sqrt d1 * sqrt d2

let pearsons = numerator / denominator

printfn "Pearsons Correlation Coefficient is %f" pearsons
```

Get the raw code at `https://gist.github.com/sudipto80/dcda6103b945bf902821`

This produces the following output:

```
Pearsons Correlation Coefficient is 0.970725
```

If two collections are exactly the same in every location, then Pearson's correlation coefficient will be exactly 1.0. You can check this by changing the elements of the arrays. This metric gives a measure of how close two collections are and if they share a positive or negative correlation. If the value of this metric is positive and close to 1, then the collections share a positive correlation. On the other hand, if the value of this metric is negative and is close to -1, then the collections share a negative correlation.

The following formula shows how Pearson's correlation coefficient is used to calculate the similarities between users, which, in turn, is used to identify the neighborhood of the user for whom the recommendations are being generated.

$$w_{u,v} = \frac{\sum_{i \in I}(r_{u,i} - \bar{r}_u)(r_{vi} - \bar{r}_v)}{\sqrt{\sum_{i \in I}(r_{u,i} - \bar{r}_u)^2}\sqrt{\sum_{i \in I}(r_{v,i} - \bar{r}_v)^2}}$$

Here, $r_{u,i}$ denotes the rating of item i given by user U. Similarly, $r_{v,i}$ denotes the rating of item i given by user v. r_u denotes the average rating given by user u to other items that they have rated. r_u denotes the average ratings given by user v to other items that they have rated. The summations are done only for those items that both users u and v have rated.

Normally, the ratings of users is given by a matrix v as shown here:

	I_1	I_2	I_3	I_4
U_1	4	?	5	5
U_2	4	2	1	
U_3	3		2	4
U_4	4	4		
U_5	2	1	3	5

The preceding matrix or table shows the ratings of four items given by five users. User 1 denoted by U_1 rated item 1 as 4. The question mark denotes the task of prediction that the recommendation system will do.

The predicted rating for item i given by user a is found by the following formula:

$$P_{a,i} = \bar{r}_a + \frac{\sum_{u \in U}(r_{u,i} - \bar{r}_u) \cdot w_{a,u}}{\sum_{u \in U}|w_{a,u}|}$$

The summation is done over the neighborhood or all the users. If the set of all users is small (such as in this case) the neighborhood can be the entire group. $\overline{r_a}$ denotes the average rating given by the user to all other items except the item i.

Implementing basic user-user collaborative filtering using F#

As you can see, there are several components in the design of user-user collaborative filtering, so it is best to write separate functions for each different component and later glue them together to get the final result.

The following function calculates the average rating given by a user to all items except a given item:

```
//Average rating for all other rated items by the user
//except the item "except"
let rBaru(u:float list)(except:int)=
    let filtered = u |> List.mapi(fun i j -> if i <> except then j else 0.0)
                     |> List.filter(fun t -> t <> 0.0)
    float ( List.sum filtered ) / float filtered.Length

//The following function finds the common item indices
let commonItemIndices (ratings:(float list)list)(a:int)(u:int)=
        List.zip  ratings.[a]  ratings.[u]
           |> List.mapi (fun index rating ->
                          if fst rating <> 0.0
                                 && snd rating <> 0.0 then index else -1 )
           |> List.filter ( fun index -> index <> -1)

//The following function returns the average of user a and u
let mu_au (ratings:(float list)list)(a:int)(u:int)=
    let com = commonItemIndices ratings a u
    let mu_a = com |> List.map (fun index ->  ratings.[a].[index]) |> List.average
    let mu_u = com |> List.map (fun index ->  ratings.[u].[index]) |> List.average
    (mu_a,mu_u)
```

Get these function definitions at `https://gist.github.com/sudipto80/7d750a446de3ff1f7f53`

The following function calculates the amount of similarity between two user's preferences using Pearson's correlation coefficient:

```
//Calculates User-User similarity using Pearson's Correlation Coefficient
let Simu (ratings:(float list)list) (a:int)(u:int)=
        //Indices of the items rated by both user a and u
        let common = commonItemIndices ratings a u
        let averages = mu_au ratings a  u
        let ra = fst averages
        let ru = snd averages
        let num = common |> List.sumBy (fun index -> (ratings.[a].[index] - ra)*
                                                     (ratings.[u].[index] - ru))
        let d1 = common |> List.sumBy (fun index -> (ratings.[a].[index] - ra)** 2.0)
        let d2 = common |> List.sumBy (fun index -> (ratings.[u].[index] - ru)** 2.0)
        //If either d1 or d2 is 0 then we shall hit a divide by zero case
        //to avoid that we must return 0.
        if d1 = 0.0 || d2 = 0.0 then 0.0 else num  / ((sqrt d1) * (sqrt d2 ))
```

By gluing all these functions together, the following function calculates the predicted value of the rating of the item i given by user a.

```
//User-User Basic Collaborative Filtering - basic
let Predictu(ratings:(float list)list)(a:int)(i:int) =
    let rb = rBaru ratings.[a] i
    let neighborIndices = ratings
                          |> List.mapi(fun index rating ->
                             if rating.[i] <> 0.0 then index else -1)
                          |> List.filter(fun index -> index <> -1)
    //Rating of neighbors are obtained
    let neighbors  = neighborIndices
                         |> List.map (fun index -> ratings.[index])
    let gaps = neighbors |> List.map (fun neighbor -> neighbor.[i] - (rBaru neighbor i))
    let simis = neighborIndices |> List.map (fun index -> Simu ratings a index)
    let num = List.zip gaps simis |> List.sumBy (fun t -> fst t * snd t)
    let den = simis |>  List.sumBy (fun similarity -> abs similarity)
    if den <> 0.0 then
       let div = num / den
       let predicted = rb + div
       //Sometimes the value of "predicted" can be beyond the range. [1-5]
       //so having a 7 is same as 5.0 in practice (meaning the user might love the item)
       //so is having a -1 which is same as 1 (meaning the user might hate the item)
       if predicted > 5.0 then 5.0 elif predicted < 1.0 then 1.0 else  predicted
    else
       0.0 //We don't know what it is.
```

Calling this function is simple, as shown below:

```
//The above rating matrix is represented as (float list)list in F#
let ratings = [[4.;0.;5.;5.];[4.;2.;1.;0.];[3.;0.;2.;4.];[4.;4.;0.;0.];[2.;1.;3.;5.]]
//Finding the predicted rating for user 1 for item 2
let p12 = Predictu  ratings  0 1
```

When these are run in F# interactive, the value of `p12` is calculated to have a value of `3.9469141902113289` or roughly `3.95`. This value can be easily converted to a 1 to 5 scale by using a ceiling call by applying the `ceil` function. However, for ranking items in a Top-N recommended item list, this actual predicted value is important.

Code walkthrough

The `commonItemIndices (ratings:(float list)list)(a:int)(u:int)` function finds item indices that have been rated by both users, a and u.

This function assumes 0 to be the default value if the value of the rating is not present or if there is a question mark. The following matrix will be useful to help you understand how this function works:

	I_1	I_2	I_3	I_4
U_1	4	?	5	5
U_2	4	2	1	
U_3	3		2	4
U_4	4	4		
U_5	2	1	3	5

Let's say that we want to find the indices of items that have been rated by both users U_1 and U_3, then **4 ? 5 5** is depicted as `[4.;0.0;5.;5.]` and **3 <space> 2 4** is depicted as `[3.;0.0;2.;4.]`

The first line of the function will be as follows:

```
List.zip  ratings.[a]  ratings.[u]
```

This zips these two collections and produces the following list of tuples:

```
[(4.,3.);(0.0,0.0);(5.,2.);(5.,4.)]
```

So, the items that have been rated by both users (U1 and U3) will be indices of those items in this zipped list where both the first and second element is non zero. The following two lines of code do that in this function:

```
|> List.mapi (fun index rating -> if fst rating <> 0.0
                                     && snd rating <> 0.0 then index else -1 )
|> List.filter ( fun index -> index <> -1)
```

The `rBaru(u:float list)(except:int)` function calculates the average rating provided by a user whose ratings are captured in the list u, except for the given item index.

The `Simu (ratings:(float list)list) (a:int)(u:int)` function calculates the similarity between the users a and u and is the implementation of the formula for $w_{u,v}$.

Finally, the `Predictu` function glues everything together to calculate the prediction of what the recommender system thinks the user might have rated item i.

If you look carefully, in the predicted item the numerator is the sum of the product of the difference in each term for user ratings and the similarity measurements. These two value sets are calculated differently and are stored in `gaps` and `simis` variables, respectively. Later, the summation of the numerator is calculated by the following command line:

```
let num = List.zip gaps simis |> List.sumBy (fun t -> fst t * snd t)
```

Here, `fst t` represents the gap and `snd t` represents the similarity. More specifically, `fst t` is the implementation of $\left(r_{u,i} - \overline{r_u}\right)$ and `snd t` is the implementation of $w_{a,u}$.

The denominator is nothing but the sum of the absolute values of all the similarity weights. This is calculated using the following line:

```
let den = simis |> List.sumBy (fun similarity -> abs similarity)
```

Variations of gap calculations and similarity measures

Although, most often, the gap is calculated by simply determining the difference between the values and their average, sometimes this can lead to scale issues where the values fall outside of the scale. Thus, there are several schemes to normalize these values. One such technique is to use the Z -score of the values.

The Z -score is defined as follows:

$$z = \frac{x - \mu}{\sigma}$$

Here, μ denotes the average and σ denotes the standard deviation. Using this formula the similarity weights can be adjusted, and the new formula for the similarity between two users using the Z -score can be represented as follows.

The following formula determines the predicted value of the rating when the Z -score is used:

$$p_{u,i} = \bar{r}_u + \sigma_u \frac{\sum_{u' \in N} s(u,u')(r_{u',i} - \bar{r}_{u'}) / \sigma_{u'}}{\sum_{u' \in N} |s(u,u')|}$$

Here $s(u,v)$ represents the similarity between the users "u" and "v". σ_u represents the standard deviation of the rating given by the user "u".

The following function calculates the standard deviation:

```
//Calculates the standard deviation
let stddev(list:float list)=
    sqrt (List.fold (fun acc elem -> acc + (float elem - List.average list) ** 2.0 ) 0.0
                    list / float list.Length)
```

And the following function calculates the Z -score from the ratings as shown below:

```
//Calculates the z-score
let zscore (ratings:(float list)list)(userIndex:int)(itemIndex:int)=
        let rBar = rBaru ratings.[userIndex] itemIndex
        let sigma = stddev ratings.[userIndex]
        ratings.[userIndex].[itemIndex] - rBar / sigma
```

Using these changes, the prediction for the rating can be calculated using the following function. Note that the entire function is the same as before; only the similarity calculation changes and the changed line is highlighted:

```
let PredictuZ(ratings:(float list)list)(a:int)(i:int) =
        let rb = rBaru ratings.[a] i
        let neighborIndices = ratings
                            |> List.mapi(fun index rating ->
                                            if rating.[i] <> 0.0
                                                  then index else -1)
                            |> List.filter(fun index -> index <> -1)
        let neighbors  = neighborIndices|> List.map (fun index -> ratings.[index])
        //This line is changed to use Z-Score instead of just the differences.
        let gaps = neighbors |> List.map (fun neighbor ->  zscore ratings a i)
        let simis = neighborIndices |> List.map (fun index -> Simu ratings a index)
        let num = List.zip gaps simis |> List.sumBy (fun t -> fst t * snd t)
        let den = simis |>  List.sumBy (fun t -> abs t)
        if den <> 0.0 then
            let div = num / den
            let predicted = rb + div * stddev ratings.[a]
            //Sometimes the value can be beyond the range.
            //so having a 7 is same as 5.0 in practice
            //so is having a -1 which is same as zero
            if predicted > 5.0 then 5.0 elif predicted < 1.0 then 1.0 else  predicted
        else
            0.0 //Else we don't know
```

When this function is used for predicting the value of the rating, it produces 5.0. Take a minute to compare. The previous implementation returned 3.95, which is roughly 4.0, and this one returns 5.0, so using the Z -score can normalize the ratings across the spectrum of possibilities (in this case, between 1.0 and 5.0).

Measuring the similarity using cosine similarity:

```
let SimuDot (ratings :(float list)list) (a:int)(u:int)=
        let num =  List.zip ratings.[a] ratings.[u]
                        |> List.sumBy (fun item -> fst item * snd item)
        let d1 = ratings.[a] |> List.sumBy (fun item -> item  * item )
        let d2 = ratings.[u] |> List.sumBy (fun item -> item  * item )

        if d1 = 0.0 || d2 = 0.0 then 0.0 else num / (sqrt d1 * sqrt d2)
```

Get the code at https://gist.github.com/sudipto80/84ea679cd85ca7f6f8c4

Item-item collaborative filtering

Like the user-user approach, items can be used to find similarities and then items can be recommended. The idea is to locate similar items based on who is purchasing them. This approach is generally taken when user bases grow. So, if the number of users is denoted by *M* and number of items is denoted by *N*, when *M* >> *N* (read: M is much greater than N) then this approach yields a good result. Most of the e-commerce sites use this algorithm to recommend items to users.

Amazon's "*People who bought this also bought these*" is a simple output of this approach. You can think of this as an inverted index of items and users in a very simple way, devoid of all the details about how ratings are persisted.

Items	Users
I1	U1,U2,U3,U5
I2	U3,U1
I3	U1,U5

Now, if a new user buys item I2, then the system will list all the other items that have been purchased by U3 and U1, which are I1 and I3. On the other hand, if the new user buys item I3, then the system will show the items purchased by U1 and U5, which are I1 and I3.

The formula used to predict the user rating in the item-based approach is as follows:

$$p_{u,i} = \frac{\sum_{j \in S} s(i,j) r_{u,j}}{\sum_{j \in S} |s(i,j)|}$$

This is the set of items that are similar to the item i

The following function finds the average rating of the item given by `itemIndex`:

```
let rBari (ratings:(float list)list)(itemIndex:int)=
    let nonZeroRatings = ratings |> List.map (fun rating -> rating.
[itemIndex])
                                          |> List.filter (fun t -> t <> 0.0)
    nonZeroRatings |> List.average
```

The following function calculates the similarity between two items using the cosine similarity measure. For the item-item approach, this metric works best.

```
let SimiDot (ratings :(float list)list)(i:int)(j:int)=
        let li = ratings |> List.map(fun rating -> rating.[i])
        let lj = ratings |> List.map(fun rating -> rating.[j])
        let num = List.zip li lj |> List.sumBy  (fun item -> fst item * snd item)
        let d1 = li |> List.sumBy (fun item -> item  * item )
        let d2 = lj |> List.sumBy (fun item -> item  * item )

        if d1 = 0.0 || d2 = 0.0 then 0.0 else num / (sqrt d1 * sqrt d2)
```

The following function glues everything together to predict user U's rating for the item i.

```
//Item based collaborative filtering - basic
let Predicti (ratings:(float list)list)(userIndex:int)(itemIndex:int)=
    let rated = ratings.[userIndex]
                       |> List.mapi (fun i t ->
                                    if t <> 0.0 then
                                              i else -1)
                       |> List.filter (fun k -> k <> -1)
    let num = rated |> List.sumBy (fun i -> ratings.[userIndex].[i] *
                                   SimiDot ratings itemIndex i)
    let den = rated |> List.sumBy ( fun i -> abs (SimiDot ratings itemIndex i) )
    let predicted = num / den
    //Predicting something as bad as -1.34 is same as predicting it as 1
    //Similarly predicting something as good as 7.5 is same as predicting it as 5
    //on a 1-5 rating scale.
    //Other than that the ranking might
    if predicted < 0.0 then 1. elif predicted > 5. then 5. else predicted
```

The ratings are predicted by this method for the same item and same user as shown here:

```
let ratings = [[4.;0.;5.;5.];[4.;2.;1.;0.];[3.;0.;2.;4.];[4.;4.;0.;0.];[2.;1.;3.;5.]]
//pre01 stands for the prediction for user 0 for item 1
let pre01 = Predicti ratings 0 1
```

The value of `pre01` is calculated to be 5.0, which is close to the ceiling value of the one calculated from the user-user approach.

The following code calculates the missing ratings for all users. The rows of the rating matrix denote the users and the columns denote the items. The following user item rating combinations were missing:

- 0,1
- 1,3
- 2,1
- 3,2
- 3,3

The following code calculates the predictions for all these using both user-user and item-item approaches:

```
let ratings = [[4.;0.;5.;5.];[4.;2.;1.;0.];[3.;0.;2.;4.];[4.;4.;0.;0.];[2.;1.;3.;5.]]
//pre01 stands for the prediction for user 0 for item 1
//pre01 stands for the prediction for user 0 and item 1
let pre01i = Predicti ratings 0 1
let pre13i = Predicti ratings 1 3
let pre21i = Predicti ratings 2 1
let pre32i = Predicti ratings 3 2
let pre33i = Predicti ratings 3 3
printfn " Item - Item Collaborative Filtering "
printfn "pre01  = %A" pre01i
printfn "pre13  = %A" pre13i
printfn "pre21  = %A" pre21i
printfn "pre32  = %A" pre32i
printfn "pre33  = %A" pre33i
let pre01u = Predictu ratings 0 1
let pre13u = Predictu ratings 1 3
let pre21u = Predictu ratings 2 1
let pre32u = Predictu ratings 3 2
let pre33u = Predictu ratings 3 3
printfn " User - User Collaborative Filtering "
```

This produces the following result:

```
Item - Item Collaborative Filtering
pre01  = 4.298436498
pre13  = 2.216813289
pre21  = 2.960973428
pre32  = 4.0
```

```
pre33  = 4.0
 User - User Collaborative Filtering


val ratings : float list list =
  [[4.0; 0.0; 5.0; 5.0]; [4.0; 2.0; 1.0; 0.0]; [3.0; 0.0; 2.0; 4.0];
   [4.0; 4.0; 0.0; 0.0]; [2.0; 1.0; 3.0; 5.0]]
val pre01i : float = 4.298436498
val pre13i : float = 2.216813289
val pre21i : float = 2.960973428
val pre32i : float = 4.0
val pre33i : float = 4.0
val pre01u : float = 3.94691419
val pre13u : float = 2.341075905
val pre21u : float = 1.774652806
val pre32u : float = 0.0
val pre33u : float = 0.0
val it : unit = ()
```

Top-N recommendations

So far, the discussion has been around prediction. A recommendation is nothing but the sorting of items based on their predicted rating values. So, for a new user who has rated a few items, the system calculates rating predictions for several items and then presents the sorted list of items based on their ratings in a descending order.

Evaluating recommendations

Understanding how good a collaborative filtering system is can be broadly determined by measuring three types of accuracy parameters, namely:

- **Prediction Accuracy Metrics**

  These measures help to understand how accurately the recommender works. These measures work by calculating the differences between previously rated items and their ratings estimated by the recommender system.

- **Decision Support Metrics (a.k.a Confusion Matrix)**

  These measures are used to find how well a supervised learning algorithm has performed.

- **Ranking Accuracy Metrics**

  These metrics are used to find out how well the recommender has placed the items in the final recommended list.

Prediction accuracy

Metrics help us to understand how good the predicted ratings are. Here are some of the prediction accuracy metrics that are used frequently:

> $p_{u,i}$ denotes the predicted rating for user u on item i. And $r_{u,i}$ is the actual rating. So the closer the value of these metrics to zero, the better the prediction algorithm.

- **MAE formula**

$$\frac{1}{n}\sum_{u,i}\left|p_{u,i}-r_{u,i}\right|$$

```
let mae (ratings:float list)(predictions:float list) =
        (List.zip ratings predictions |> List.sumBy (fun t -> abs (fst t - snd t)))
                        /float ratings.Length
```

- **NMAE formula**

$$\frac{1}{n\left(r_{high}-r_{low}\right)}\sum_{u,i}\left|p_{u,i}-r_{u,i}\right|$$

```
//Normalized Mean Absolute Error
let nmae (ratings:float list)(predictions:float list) =
   let rMax = ratings |> List.max
   let rMin = ratings |> List.min
   (mae ratings predictions )/(rMax - rMin)
```

- **RMSE formula**

$$\sqrt{\frac{1}{n}\sum_{u,i}\left(p_{u,i}-r_{u,i}\right)^2}$$

```
//Root mean squared error
let rmse(ratings:float list)(predictions:float list) =
    sqrt( ( List.zip ratings predictions
                |> List.map (fun t -> fst t - snd t)
                     |> List.sum )
         /(float predictions.Length ))
```

You can find the raw code of all these methods defined at
`https://gist.github.com/sudipto80/8fc75f804e04d80b15c7`

As an exercise, you can perform all kinds of variations to the algorithms as described in this chapter and then create a table of values with these evaluation metrics.

Confusion matrix (decision support)

Supervised learning algorithms routinely fail at the task of classifying and these algorithms confuse one type of object for the other. The better the algorithm gets, the less confused it will be. The name **Confusion Matrix** stems from this fact. A confusion matrix is a combination of several metrics that help users to understand how well the algorithm is performing.

Here are the different metrics:

- True positive (TP)

  Eqv. with hit

- True negative (TN)

  Eqv. with correct rejection

- False positive (FP)

  Eqv. with false alarm, Type I error

- False negative (FN)

  Eqv. with miss, Type II error

- Sensitivity or true positive rate (TPR)
  Eqv. with hit rate, recall

$$TPR = \frac{TP}{P} = \frac{TP}{TP + FN}$$

- Specificity (SPC) or true negative rate (TNR)

$$SPC = \frac{TN}{N} = \frac{TN}{FP + TN}$$

- Precision or positive predictive value (PPV)

$$PPV = \frac{TP}{TP + FP}$$

- Negative predictive value (NPV)

$$NPV = \frac{TN}{TN + FN}$$

- Fall-out or false positive rate (FPR)

$$FPR = \frac{FP}{N} = \frac{FP}{FP + TN} = 1 - SPC$$

- False discovery rate (FDR)

$$FDR = \frac{FP}{FP + TP} = 1 - PPV$$

- Miss rate or false negative rate (FNR)

$$FNR = \frac{FN}{P} = \frac{FN}{FN + TP}$$

- Accuracy (ACC)

$$ACC = \frac{TP + TN}{P + N}$$

- F1 score, which is the harmonic mean of precision and sensitivity

$$F1 = \frac{2TP}{2TP + FP + FN}$$

- Matthews correlation coefficient (MCC)

$$\frac{TP \times TN - FP \times FN}{\sqrt{(TP + FP)(TP + FN)(TN + FP)(TN + FN)}}$$

If a classification system has been trained to distinguish between cats, dogs, and rabbits, a confusion matrix will summarize the results of testing the algorithm for further inspection. Assuming a sample of 27 animals, 8 cats, 6 dogs, and 13 rabbits, the resulting confusion matrix will look like the following table:

		Predicted		
		Cat	**Dog**	**Rabbit**
Actual class	Cat	5	3	0
	Dog	2	3	1
	Rabbit	0	2	11

In this confusion matrix, of the eight actual cats, the system predicted that three were dogs and, of the six dogs, it predicted that one was a rabbit and two were cats. We can see from the matrix that the system in question has trouble distinguishing between cats and dogs, but can make the distinction between rabbits and other types of animals pretty well. All correct guesses are located in the diagonal of the table, so it's easy to visually inspect the table for errors, as they will be represented by values outside the diagonal.

The following code implements some of these metric definitions. The matrix is represented as a 2D array of integers.

```
module confusion =
    let TP (matches : int [] []) =
        matches |> Array.mapi( fun i j -> matches.[i].[i]) |> Array.sum

    //True Positive for entries correctly identified of type "thisOne"
    let TP_for (thisOne : int) (matches : int [] []) =
        matches.[thisOne].[thisOne]

    //False positive for
    let FP_for (thisOne : int) (matches : int [] []) =
        let all = [for i in 0 .. matches.Length-1 -> matches.[i].[thisOne]]
        let allSum = all |> List.sum
        allSum - (TP_for thisOne matches)

    //False negative for
    let FN_for (thisOne : int) (matches : int [] []) =
        let all = [for  i in 0 .. matches.[thisOne].Length - 1 -> matches.[thisOne].[i]]
        let allSum = all |> List.sum
        allSum - matches.[thisOne].[thisOne]

    //F1
    let F1(thisOne : int) (matches : int [] []) =
        2. * float (TP_for thisOne matches) /
        ( 2. * float (TP_for thisOne matches) + float( FP_for thisOne matches )+ float (FN_for thisOne matches))
```

You can download the entire module from
https://github.com/sudipto80/Measures/blob/master/confusion.fs

Although there are several metrics, an easy way to interpret the outcome of a supervised learning algorithm, in this case the predicted rating (if it was a recommendation the user picked), is to check the F1-score. The F1-score ranges from 0 to 1. The closer to 1 it is, the better is the performance of the system.

The following code uses the methods described earlier to calculate the F1 scores for cat, dog, and rabbit matches.

```
open confusion
let matches = [|[|5;3;0|];[|2;3;1|];[|0;2;11|]|]
let cat = 0
let dog = 1
let rabbit = 2

let catF1 = F1 cat matches
let dogF1 = F1 dog matches
let rabbitF1 = F1 rabbit matches
```

This means that the accuracy of identifying `rabbits` was 88% while that of identifying `dogs` was only 43%, roughly.

In a setting where recommendations are provided and users have an option to select from the first few recommended items, a confusion matrix can be provided to capture the user's feedback about whether they had chosen a recommendation or not. If a user had chosen to take an action based on the recommendation, then that recommendation can be thought to be a successful scenario, else the outcome of the recommendation system is a failure. Based on these, a confusion matrix can be obtained that captures the total number of times the system generated recommendations were accepted, and the total number of times they were rejected.

Ranking accuracy metrics

A third view of the task of a recommender system is that it ranks all items with respect to a user (or ranks all user-item pairs), such that the higher-ranked recommendations are more likely to be relevant to users. Individual rating predictions may be incorrect, but, as long as the order is caught correctly, rank accuracy measures will evaluate the system as having a high accuracy.

Prediction-rating correlation

If the variance of one variable can be explained by the variance in another, the two variables are said to correlate. Let $s_1, \ldots, s_n$ be items and $u_1, \ldots, u_n$ be their true order rank. Let the recommender system predict the ranks $u_1^p, \ldots, u_n^p$ for these items (i.e., u_i is the true rank of the item and u_i^p is the predicted rank). Let $\overline{u}$ be the mean of $u_1, \ldots, u_n$, and $\overline{u}^p$ be the mean of $u_1^p, \ldots, u_n^p$. The Spearman's correlation is defined as follows:

$$\rho = \frac{\sum_{i=1} \left(u_i - \overline{u}\right)\left(u_i^p - \overline{u}^p\right)}{n \cdot stdev\left(u\right) \cdot stdev\left(u^p\right)}$$

The following code finds the coefficient:

```
let trueRanks = [1.;2.;3.;4.;5.;5.;7.;8.;9.;10.]
let predictedRanks = [1.;2.;3.;4.;6.;7.;5.;8.;10.;9.]
let uBar  =  trueRanks  |> List.average

let upBar = predictedRanks |> List.average

let stdevTrue  = stddev trueRanks
let stdevPredicted = stddev predictedRanks

let n = 10.

let numerator = List.zip trueRanks predictedRanks
                |> List.map (fun item -> (float (fst item) - uBar) * (float (snd item) - upBar))
                |> List.sum

let denominator = n * stdevTrue * stdevPredicted

let p = numerator /denominator
```

Get the raw code at `https://gist.github.com/sudipto80/89253a340503f7559cce`

This produces the following output:

```
val p : float = 0.9338995047
```

This means that the recommender is 93% correct in laying out the top N recommendations. Suppose you reverse the order of the predicted ranks as shown here:

```
let predictedRanks = [10.;9.;8.;7.;6.;5.;4.;3.;2.;1.]
```

This will give you a negative correlation, which means that the recommender did a miserable job of laying out the top N recommendations.

```
val p : float = -0.9945423296
```

Working with real movie review data (Movie Lens)

You can download the Movie Lens 100K dataset (for collaborative filtering) from `http://files.grouplens.org/datasets/movielens/ml-100k/`.

This dataset has movie ratings given by 943 users for 1,682 movies. These ratings are stored in the `u.data` file at `http://files.grouplens.org/datasets/movielens/ml-100k/u.data`. The full *u* data set has 100,000 ratings by 943 users on 1,682 items.

Each user has rated at least 20 movies. The users and items are numbered consecutively from 1. The data is randomly ordered. This is a tab separated list of:

user id | item id | rating | timestamp.

The time stamps are in Unix seconds since 1/1/1970 UTC.

The following C# program translates this data to an F# array so that this data can be fed to the collaborative filtering algorithms implemented earlier in the chapter:

`https://gist.github.com/sudipto80/606418978f4a86fe93aa`

Once you generate this array, you can then plug this into the algorithms described earlier.

Summary

In this chapter, the most commonly used memory-based approaches for recommendations were discussed. There are several other approaches to recommender system building, which have not been discussed here, such as model-based and hybrid recommendations systems that take cues from several other recommendation algorithms to produce final recommendations. However, We hope this chapter gave you a nice introduction and hands-on guide to implementations for these collaborative filtering ideas. All source code is available at `https://gist.github.com/sudipto80/7002e66350ca7b2a7551`.

6
Sentiment Analysis

"Are you happy or not; that's the question!"

Sentiment Analysis (**SA**) or opinion mining is a technique used to figure out the polarity (positivity or negativity) of a sentence automatically.

This can be quite difficult given that natural language is difficult for computers to decipher. There is another related concept called **Emotion Detection** (**ED**). While the task of SA is to determine whether a given sentence or a phrase represents a positive or negative sentiment, ED tries to do something more challenging. It tries to find the actual emotion being expressed in a text.

So, the output of ED algorithms is categorical (joy, sadness, anger, violence, feel-good) while that of SA algorithms is mostly Boolean (the sentence being examined by the algorithm has either a positive or a negative polarity).

Sometimes, it makes sense to return the polarity percentage from SA algorithms as that can be used as a degree of positivity. SA is important because it gives companies the power to track public sentiment about a product or a service that they are providing. So, if the general public sentiment is bad (negative polarity), then companies can do something about it because they can now see the data.

Objective

After reading this chapter, you will be able to understand how some of the sites recommend items based on your item browsing history and what you have rated. You will understand the mathematics behind collaborative filtering and how these can be applied to your problem domain. All source code is available at `https://gist.github.com/sudipto80/6121c3eb47698c4f3b4c`.

What you will learn

You will learn about the jargon of the industry when experts are speaking about Sentiment Analysis. You will find complete implementations of a couple of algorithms used to identify the polarity that you can use almost as-is in your domain.

A baseline algorithm for SA using SentiWordNet lexicons

Sentiment Analysis algorithms work by referring external resources where the positive and negative polarity of each word is considered. These external words, for which the polarity is predetermined, are known as lexicons. There are several lists of lexicons available and each one focuses on the polarity of a given word in a particular context. For example, consider the following couple of sentences:

- The play has an unpredictable plot
- This car's steering is unpredictable

The first usage of *unpredictable* indicates that the play is good. If this statement is found on an online portal that lets users rate plays, then this phrase can be taken as a positive feedback for the play involved. On the other hand, the usage of *unpredictable* in the second sentence means that driving the car could be dangerous because the steering wheel is unpredictable in its functioning. Thus, if we use a general-purpose lexicon that has a high negative polarity for the word *unpredictable*, then both of these phrases will have a negative polarity. In other words, the system will conclude that users are expressing negative emotions using these two sentences. However, as you know, unpredictability in the plot of a play is great while unpredictability in a car's steering wheel is not. Thus, the first phrase leads to a positive sentiment while the second one doesn't.

You can download the SentiWordNet list from `http://sentiwordnet.isti.cnr.it/`.

The algorithm is simple. For all words that are lexicons, the positivity (positive polarity) and negativity (negative polarity) are calculated and then summed up. If the positivity is high, then the sentence from which the words have been extracted is thought to have a positive polarity; otherwise the sentence is believed to have a negative polarity. The absolute value is considered to be the degree of positive or negative polarity present in the sentence.

SentiWordNet is a text file where the entries (read: each row of a lexicon) look like the following:

```
a   00158701   0.125   0   affixed#1   firmly attached; "the affixed
labels"
```

The first column stands for the part of speech (*a* is for adjective) of the given lexicon. The second element in the row is the ID of the lexicon. The third column represents the positive polarity of the lexicon (In this case the word *affixed*) and the fourth column represents the negative polarity of the lexicon. The fourth column shows a few synonyms by adding the # suffix to those and then follows a long meaning of the phrase.

The following functions use SentiWordNet to find out the polarity of a given sentence or phrase.

This line loads all the SentiWordNet entries in a strongly typed array, where the type is represented by the following:

```
type SentiWordNetEntry = {POS:string; ID:string; PositiveScore:string; NegativeScore:string; Words:string}
```

This type maps each row of the SentiWordNet file:

```
let sentiWordList = System.IO.File.ReadAllLines(@"SentiWordNet_3.0.0_20130122.txt")
                                |> Array.filter (fun line -> not (line.StartsWith("#")))
                                |> Array.map (fun line -> line.Split '\t')
                                |> Array.map (fun lineTokens -> {POS = lineTokens.[0];
                                                                 ID = lineTokens.[1];
                                                                 PositiveScore = lineTokens.[2].Trim();
                                                                 NegativeScore = lineTokens.[3].Trim();
                                                                 Words = lineTokens.[4]})

                                |> Array.map(fun item ->  [item.Words.Substring(0,item.Words.LastIndexOf('#')+1);
                                                           item.PositiveScore;item.NegativeScore])
```

In the following section, I have captured a portion of the output of these lines in `F#` interactive so that you can see what constitutes this list. It is an array of string lists where the first element of each list represents the words, the second element represents the positive polarity, and the third element represents the negative polarity of the word or all the words that appear in the first element of the list. For example, `able` has a positive polarity of `0.125` and `unable` has a negative polarity of `0.75`.

```
val sentiWordList : string list [] =
  [|["able#"; "0.125"; "0"]; ["unable#"; "0"; "0.75"];
    ["dorsal#2 abaxial#"; "0"; "0"]; ["ventral#2 adaxial#"; "0"; "0"];
    ["acroscopic#"; "0"; "0"]; ["basiscopic#"; "0"; "0"];
```

```
        ["abducting#1 abducent#"; "0"; "0"];
        ["adductive#1 adducting#1 adducent#"; "0"; "0"]; ["nascent#"; "0";
"0"];
        ["emerging#2 emergent#"; "0"; "0"]; ["dissilient#"; "0.25"; "0"];
        ["parturient#"; "0.25"; "0"]; ["dying#"; "0"; "0"];
        ["moribund#"; "0"; "0"]; ["last#"; "0"; "0"]; ["abridged#"; "0";
"0"];
        ["shortened#4 cut#"; "0"; "0"]; ["half-length#"; "0"; "0"];
        ["potted#"; "0"; "0"]; ["unabridged#"; "0"; "0"];
```

This function returns the absolute polarity of a given word:

```
let getPolarity (sentiWordNetList:string list[]) (word:string) =
    let matchedItem = sentiWordNetList
                      |> Array.filter(fun item -> item.[0].Contains (word))

    match matchedItem.Length  with
        | 0 -> (0.0,0.0)//No value found
        //There can be multiple match; picking the first one (i.e: matchedItem.[0])
        | _ -> (float matchedItem.[0].[1], float matchedItem.[0].[2])
```

This function returns the absolute polarity of a given phrase by calculating the polarity of each word and then summing up those results. If the total positive polarity of the words is more than that of the total negative polarity, then this function returns `1` (indicating an overall positive polarity). However, if both are the same, then it returns `0` (indicating a neutral polarity); otherwise, it returns `-1` (indicating an overall negative polarity).

```
let getPolarityScore (sentence:string) (sentiWordNetList:string list[]) =
    let words = sentence.Split ' '
    let mutable totalPositivity = 0.0
    let mutable totalNegativity = 0.0
    let polarities  = words
                      |> Array.map(fun word -> getPolarity sentiWordNetList word)
    polarities
              |> Array.map (fun polarity -> totalPositivity <- totalPositivity + fst polarity)
              |> ignore

    polarities
              |> Array.map (fun polarity -> totalNegativity <- totalNegativity + snd polarity)
              |> ignore

    if totalPositivity > totalNegativity then 1  //Positive polarity
    elif totalNegativity = totalPositivity then 0  //Neutral polarity
    else -1 //Negative polarity
```

The following lines were run in F# interactive:

```
//Finding polarities of the sentences using SentiWordNet
getPolarityScore "I am loving this product.I thought that the camera will be much better" sentiWordList
getPolarityScore "don't buy this drug . it gave me a bummer" sentiWordList //negative
```

The following was the output:

```
>
val it : int = 1
>
val it : int = -1
```

This means that the sentiment being expressed through the first sentence is positive, while the sentiment being expressed in the second sentence is negative.

Handling negations

Sometimes, positive and negative polarities balance each other and a sentence for which you would expect to get a negative polarity ends up being an objective statement (meaning that the sentence doesn't have a polarity at all).

Consider the following sentence:

- The camera of the phone was not good

The positive polarity of this sentence is calculated to be `0.625` (because of the word `good`) and the negative polarity of the sentence is calculated to be `0.625` (because of the word `not`). Thus, the overall polarity of this document is calculated to be zero; or in other words, the document is said to have no polarity at all. But as humans, we know that this phrase echoes a negative sentiment because the user is saying that the camera of the phone is not good.

In this section, we will see how we can tweak the above implementation to suit this type of sentence case.

The basic idea is to penalize a good word's positivity score with the value of the preceding negative words negative score using a penalizing score. In the preceding example, `not` is a negative word that precedes a positive word `good`. So, instead of scoring them separately, if they have to be treated together as `not good` and if all such pairs (that are joined by an underscore and start with a negative word, such as not, nor, neither, never, seldom, and so on) are scored using the penalizing factor, then the overall polarity of the sentence will be affected by the negative forerunners of the good words.

To do this, at first all the positive words (for which the positive polarity is more than the negative polarity) and all the negative words (for which the negative polarity is more than the positive polarity) have to be found.

The following functions find positive and negative words:

```
let allPositiveWords (sentiWordNetList:string list[])=
    sentiWordNetList
      |> Array.filter(fun sentiWord ->  float sentiWord.[1] > float sentiWord.[2])
      |> Array.map (fun sentiWord -> sentiWord.[0])

let allNegativeWords (sentiWordNetList:string list[])=
    sentiWordNetList
      |> Array.filter(fun sentiWord ->  float sentiWord.[1] < float sentiWord.[2])
      |> Array.map (fun sentiWord -> sentiWord.[0])
```

There can be more than one word with the same polarity or a similar meaning such as in this case. Some of the rest of the line is depicted by the ellipsis (...) due to space concerns.

```
r  00024073  0  0.625  not#1 non#1  negation of a word or group of
words; .."

let positiveWords = allPositiveWords z |> Array.toList
let negativeWords = allNegativeWords z |> Array.toList

let delims = [|'#';' '|]
let pos = positiveWords |> List.map (fun t -> t.Split delims
                                             |> Array.filter
                                             (fun z -> Regex.Match(z,"[a-
zA-Z]+").Success))

let neg = negativeWords |> List.map (fun t -> t.Split delims
                                             |> Array.filter
                                             (fun z -> Regex.Match(z,"[a-
zA-Z]+").Success))

let mutable posList = [""]
let mutable negList = [""]

pos |> List.map (fun current -> [for k in 0 .. current.Length - 1 ->
                                            posList <- posList @
[current.[k]]])
      |> ignore
```

```
neg |> List.map (fun current -> [for k in 0 .. current.Length - 1 ->
                                                      negList <- negList @
[current.[k]]])
    |> ignore

posList <- posList |> List.filter (fun word -> word.Length > 0)
negList <- negList |> List.filter (fun word -> word.Length > 0)
```

The key idea is to locate negation words followed by a positive word and replace them with a predetermined placeholder (in this case, `Negative_detected` is used) and also to find negation words followed by a negative word and replace them with a predetermined placeholder (`Ok_detected` in this case). This is because when people express negative sentiments they generally write a positive word followed by a negation word such as `not good`. On the other hand, `the phone is not bad` (note that `bad`, which is a negatively polarized word, is being followed by another negation word `not`) expresses a somewhat positive (kind of OK) sentiment.

To cater for this need, the `getPolarity` function has to be changed as shown in the following code. The modified part is highlighted.

```
let getPolarity (sentiWordNetList:string list[]) (word:string) =
    let wordWithHash = String.concat "" [word; "#"]
    let wordWithLeadingBlankAndHash = String.concat "" [" ";wordWithHash]
    let matchedItem = sentiWordNetList
                    |> Array.filter(fun item -> item.[0].ToString().StartsWith(wordWithHash)
                                                 || item.[0].ToString().Contains wordWithLeadingBlankAndHash)

    match matchedItem.Length  with
        | 0 -> if word = "Negative_detected" then (0.0,0.675)
               elif word = "Ok_detected" then (0.125,0.0)
               else (0.0,0.0)//No value found
        //There can be multiple match
        | _ -> (float matchedItem.[0].[1], float matchedItem.[0].[2])
```

The following lines create Cartesian products of negations and bad and good words, creating combinations that people use to express somewhat positive (`okCombos`) and negative sentiments (`badCombos`):

```
let negations = ["no";"not";"never";"seldom";"neither";"nor"]
let badCombos = negations
              |> List.collect (fun x -> posList |> List.map (fun y -> x + " " + y))
let okCombos = negations
              |> List.collect (fun x -> negList |> List.map (fun y -> x + " " + y))
```

Here are some of the items from `badCombos` and `okCombos`

```
val badCombos : string list =
  ["no able"; "no dissilient"; "no parturient"; "no uncut"; "no full-
length";
   "no absolute"; "no direct"; "no infinite"; "no living"; "no
sorbefacient";
   "no absorbefacient"; "no absorbable"; "no adsorbate"; "no
adsorbable";
   "no spartan"; "no austere"; "no ascetical"; "no ascetic"; "no
notional";
   ...]
val okCombos : string list =
  ["no unable"; "no relative"; "no comparative"; "no assimilatory";
   "no assimilative"; "no assimilating"; "no receptive"; "no
nonabsorptive";
   "no nonabsorbent"; "no resistant"; "no repellent"; "no
chemosorptive";
   "no unappreciated"; "no unconfessed"; "no unrecognized"; "no
unrecognised";
   "no voracious"; "no ravening"; "no rapacious"; ...]
```

The last step is to replace such bad combo pairs with `Negative_detected` and ok combo pairs with `Ok_detected` placeholders. The following two lines perform this trick:

```
let mutable sen = "the camera of the phone was not amazing"
badCombos |> List.map (fun badWordCombo -> sen <- Regex.Replace (sen, badWordCombo,"Negative_detected"))
          |> ignore
okCombos |> List.map (fun badWordCombo -> sen <- Regex.Replace (sen, badWordCombo,"Ok_detected"))
         |> ignore
```

After these modifications, the polarity score is calculated again:

```
getPolarityScore sen sentiWordList
```

This time, the polarity is reported as `-1`, as shown here:

```
val it : int = -1
```

This means that the system now correctly tags the sentence as having a negative polarity.

Identifying praise or criticism with sentiment orientation

The evaluative character of a word is called its semantic orientation. Positive semantic orientation indicates praise (for example, `honest`, `intrepid`) and negative semantic orientation indicates criticism (for example, `disturbing`, `superfluous`). Semantic orientation varies in both direction (positive or negative) and degree (mild to strong). An automated system for measuring semantic orientation will have its application in text classification, text filtering, tracking opinions in online discussions, analysis of survey responses, and automated chat systems (chatbots).

Semantic Orientation (**SO**) is used to determine whether a particular phrase is praising or criticizing someone or something. Turney and Littman proposed an algorithm for determining that using SO.

If the SO of the phrase is positive then the phrase is thought to have a positive sentiment; in other words, the phrase is said to be praising. Otherwise, if the SO value of the phrase is negative then the phrase is thought to have a negative sentiment; in other words, the phrase is said to criticize someone or something.

So of a word `word1` with another word `word2` is a way to estimate how likely a word `word1` will occur with `word2`. If `word2` is a positive word and the semantic orientation of `word1` is high with `word2`, it means that `word1` is also a positive word. On the contrary, if `word2` is a negative word then a strong semantic orientation with `word2` will mean that `word1` is also a negative word.

The general strategy for finding a semantic orientation is as follows:

$$SO(w) = \sum_{w_p \in positive-words} A(w, w_p) - \sum_{w_n \in negative-words} A(w, w_n)$$

$A(word1, word2)$ is the strategy to determine orientation. Positive and negative-words are as follows:

Positive-words are: `good`, `nice`, `excellent`, `positive`, `fortunate`, `correct`, `superior`.

Negative-words are: `bad`, `nasty`, `poor`, `negative`, `unfortunate`, `wrong`, `inferior`.

W_p denotes each positive word and W_n denotes each negative word. There are several choices of $A(word1, word2)$ that one can make resulting in several possible implementation of the SO scheme. But the PMI (Pointwise Mutual Information metric) gives the best result. Using PMI as $A(\ )$ gives a special name to this scheme and it is called **Semantic Orientation Detection using Pointwise Mutual Information (SO-PMI)**.

Pointwise Mutual Information

PMI between two words is calculated using the following formula:

$$PMI(word_1, word_2) = \log_2\left(\frac{p(word_1 \,\&\, word_2)}{p(word_1)\,p(word_2)}\right)$$

$p(word)$ represent the number of occurrences of the word `word` in the entire document collection. The original article that proposed this idea used the number of articles returned for the search word `word` from the AltaVista search engine. But you can safely use a probability (the number of documents in which the word `word` appeared divided by the total number of documents). The `&` operator in $p(word_1 \,\&\, word_2)$ refers to the number of documents containing both words `word1` and `word2` divided by the total number of documents.

The following function finds the probability of the word in a document collection represented by `list`:

```
let prob list word =
    let matchCount =  list |> List.filter (fun z -> z |> List.contains word)
                                                         |> List.length |> float
    matchCount / float list.Length
```

The following function finds the probability of the words `w1` and `w2` in a document collection represented by `list`:

```
let probBoth list w1 w2 =
    let matchCount = list |>List.filter (fun z -> z |> List.contains w1 && z |> List.contains w2 )
                          |>List.length |> float
    matchCount / float list.Length
```

The following function calculates the PMI between `w1` and `w2`:

```
let pmi docs w1 w2 =
    let numerator = probBoth docs w1 w2
    let denominator = (prob docs w1) * (prob docs w2)
    if denominator > 0.0 && numerator > 0.0 then log (numerator / denominator) else 0.0
```

Using SO-PMI to find sentiment analysis

The following code finds the semantic orientation of a list of words. The variable `posi` holds the total positive semantic orientation while the variable `negi` holds the total negative semantic orientation. If `posi` is greater than `negi` then the phrase (comprising these words) is considered to have a positive polarity; otherwise it is considered to have a negative sentiment.

```
//List of positive words
let pWords = ["good"; "nice"; "excellent"; "positive"; "fortunate";
              "correct"; "superior"]

//List of negative words
let nWords = ["bad"; "nasty"; "poor"; "negative"; "unfortunate"; "wrong"; "inferior"]
let mutable posi = 0.0 //Total positive semantic orientation
let mutable negi = 0.0 //Total negative semantic orientation

let docs =[
            [["positive";"outlook"];["good";"service"];["nice";"people"];["bad";"location"]];//Bank1
            [["nasty";"behaviour"];["unfortunate"; "outcome"];["poor";"quality"]]//Bank2
          ]
for i in 0 .. docs.Length - 1 do
    for j in 0 .. docs.[i].Length - 1    do
        for pw in pWords do
            posi <- posi + pmi docs docs.[i].[j] pw

for i in 0 .. docs.Length - 1 do
    for j in 0 .. docs.[i].Length - 1    do
        for pw in nWords do
            negi <- negi + pmi docs docs.[i].[j] pw

let so_pmi = posi - negi //Calculating semantic orientation's value
```

The following function encapsulates the logic above such that it can be called with `pWords` and `nWords` from a function (`soPMI`) that calculates the semantic orientation values for each element in a review.

```
let calculateSO (docs:string list list)(words:string list)=
    let mutable res  = 0.0
    for i in 0 .. docs.Length - 1 do
        for j in 0 .. docs.[i].Length - 1    do
            for pw in words do
                res <- res + pmi docs docs.[i].[j] pw
    res
```

The function `soPMI` calculates semantic orientation for each of the reviews. Each review is represented as a list of words as shown below. Let's say that the first element of the reviews list represents the review about a bank called `Bank1` and the second element represents the list of review items for the review of a bank called `Bank2`:

```
let soPMI ( reviews : string list list list )=
    let mutable posi = 0.0
    let mutable negi = 0.0
    reviews |> List.map (fun docs ->
                    posi <- calculateSO docs pWords
                    negi <- calculateSO docs nWords
                    (docs,   posi - negi))
```

The following call calculates semantic orientation for all the reviews in the list of reviews; in this case, there are two reviews for two banks.

```
soPMI reviews

The above call produces the following result in F# interactive.

val it : (string list list * float) list =
  [([["positive"; "outlook"]; ["good"; "service"]; ["nice"; "people"];
     ["bad"; "location"]], 5.545177444);
   ([["nasty"; "behaviour"]; ["unfortunate"; "outcome"]; ["poor";
"quality"]],
    -6.591673732)]
```

I have highlighted the value of semantic orientation. As you can see, the first review has a positive semantic orientation. This means that a positive sentiment is being expressed by those reviews about `Bank1`. The semantic orientation value of the second review is negative and thus it represents that the review is expressing a negative sentiment. In other words, the first review is *praising* the target (in this case `Bank1`) of the sentiment, while in the second review is *criticizing* the target (in this case `Bank2`)

Summary

Sentiment Analysis is a very active area of research right now. There are several aspects about this task that makes it very hard. In this chapter, the basic techniques have been discussed. However, sometimes the positive sentiment can be negatively perceived. For example, if someone is checking the public sentiment for a political figure then any statement with a positive sentiment towards an opponent of the political figure in question should actually be treated as a negative sentiment. Also, identifying sarcasm in phrases can be very challenging and that can lead to an increase in a false positive rate. Moreover, identifying the target of the sentiment automatically can be quite challenging. For example, consider the following statement *the food was great but the décor was old-fashioned*. If this statement appears for a website that rates restaurants, then identifying the sentiment towards *food* as positive but that for décor (another possible feature in the restaurant entity) as negative, is quite challenging.

7
Anomaly Detection

"Find the odd one out automatically."

Anomaly Detection is the art of finding the odd one out in a bunch of data automatically. As the name suggests, it is the science of finding the data that is anomalous compared to the other. However, there are several kinds of anomalies; sometimes the normal (non-anomalous) data can be line anomalous data. Anomaly detection is mostly an unsupervised learning problem because it is very difficult, if not impossible, to get a labeled training dataset that is anomalous. Sometimes, anomalies are referred to as "outliers."

Objective

After reading this chapter, you will be able to apply some of the techniques to identify any anomaly in data, and you will have a general understanding of how and where anomaly detection algorithms can be useful. All code is available at `https://gist.github.com/sudipto80/e599ab069981736ffa1d`.

Different classification algorithms

The following algorithms will be discussed in this chapter:

- Statistical anomaly detection
- Nearest neighbor based anomaly detection
- Density estimation based anomaly detection

Some cool things you will do

With the techniques learned from this chapter, you will be able to spot lies. You will also have a deeper understanding of how fraudulent behaviors on credit cards are found.

The different types of anomalies

Anomalies can be classified into any of the following categories:

- Point anomalies
- Contextual anomalies
- Collective anomalies

We will go through each one of them in detail:

- **Point anomalies**: If an individual data instance can be considered as anomalous with respect to the rest of the data, then the instance is termed as a point anomaly. This is the simplest type of anomaly and is the focus of the majority of research in anomaly detection. The good news is that other types of anomalies can sometimes be represented as point anomalies and, thus, algorithms that are geared to find point anomalies can be useful in several other situations.

  A real life example of point anomaly detection is identifying fraudulent credit card transactions. Let's say that we have data about a subject's credit card expenditure in terms of the amount spent on each transaction. An instance with a very high figure of money spent compared to the rest of the data can be tagged as an anomaly. The algorithms covered in this chapter will deal with this type of anomaly detection.

- **Contextual anomalies**: If a data instance is anomalous in a specific context, but not otherwise, then it is called contextual anomaly. This is sometimes referred to as a conditional anomaly. Contextual anomalies are described based on the following two attributes:
  - **Contextual attributes**: These attributes are used to determine the context (or neighborhood) for that instance. For example, in spatial datasets, the longitude and latitude of a location are contextual attributes.
  - **Behavioral attributes**: The behavioral attributes define the non-contextual characteristics of the data instance. For example, in a spatial dataset describing the average rainfall of the entire world, the amount of rainfall at any location is the behavioral attribute.

The anomalous behavior is determined using the values for the behavioral attributes within a specific context.

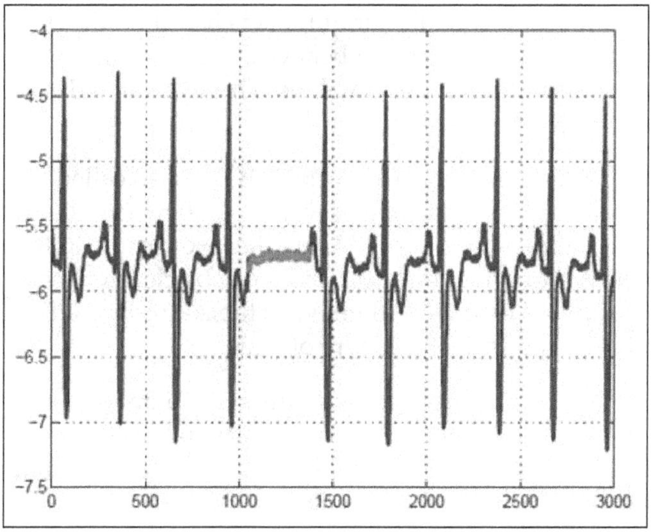

- **Collective anomalies**: If a collection of related data instances is anomalous with respect to the entire dataset, it is termed as a collective anomaly. The individual data instances in a collective anomaly might not be anomalies by themselves, but their occurrence together as a collection is anomalous. The preceding figure illustrates an example that shows the electrocardiogram output of a human being. The highlighted region denotes an anomaly because the same low value exists for an abnormally long time (corresponding to an **Atrial Premature Contraction**). Note that this low value by itself is not an anomaly.

Note that, while point anomalies can occur in any dataset, collective anomalies can only occur in datasets in which data instances are related. In contrast, the occurrence of contextual anomalies depends on the availability of contextual attributes in the data. A point anomaly or a collective anomaly can also be a contextual anomaly if analyzed with respect to a context. Thus, a point anomaly detection problem or collective anomaly detection problem can be transformed into a contextual anomaly detection problem by incorporating the context information.

In this chapter, we will discuss some well-known algorithms for the detection of anomalies or outliers using statistical methods. Anomaly detection is mostly treated as an unsupervised learning problem because getting labeled data for anomalous entries can be very expensive. Moreover, the labeled data for anomalous entries may not remain representative over time.

Detecting point anomalies using IQR (Interquartile Range)

The basic algorithm to find anomalies or outliers is based on the quartile range. The basic idea behind this approach is that it believes that elements falling far off both sides of the normal distribution are anomalous. These far-off sides are determined by the boundaries of the box plot.

In descriptive statistics, the **interquartile range** (**IQR**), also called the midspread or middle fifty, is a measure of statistical dispersion equal to the difference between the upper and lower quartiles, $IQR = Q3 - Q1$. In other words, the IQR is the 1st quartile subtracted from the 3rd quartile; these quartiles can be clearly seen on a box plot in the data. It is a trimmed estimator, defined as the 25% trimmed range, and is the most significant, basic, and robust measure of scale.

The interquartile range is often used to find outliers in data. Outliers are observations that fall below Q1 - 1.5(IQR) or above Q3 + 1.5(IQR). In a boxplot, the highest and lowest occurring values within this limit are drawn as whiskers on the bar, whereas the outliers are denoted by individual points.

Q1 and Q3 are calculated to be the medians of the smaller items (those smaller than the median of the entire list) and the bigger items (those bigger than the median of the entire list).

The following methods find the median of the IQR range, and then the `findOutliers` method uses these two functions to find the indices of the elements where anomalous elements occur:

```
//Finds the median
let median numbers =
     let sorted =  List.sort numbers
     let n = float numbers.Length
     let x = int (n/2.)
     let mutable result = 0.0
     if (float numbers.Length) % 2. = 0.0 then result <- float (numbers.[x] +
                                                     numbers.[x-1]) / 2.0
                                          else result <- float numbers.[x]
     result
//Finds the inter quartile range
let getIQRRange numbers  =
    let med = median numbers
    let smaller = numbers |> List.filter (fun item -> item < med)
    let bigger  = numbers |> List.filter (fun item -> item > med)
    let q1 = median smaller
    let q3 = median bigger
    let iqr = q3 - q1
    (q1-1.5 * iqr, q3 + 1.5*iqr )
```

```
//Find the indices where the outliers occur
let findOutliers numbers =
    let iqrRange = getIQRRange numbers
    numbers |> List.mapi (fun index item -> if item < fst iqrRange || item > snd iqrRange
                                                                then index else -1)
            |> List.filter (fun index -> index <> -1)
```

The following input is given:

```
findOutliers [2.;3.;4.;5.;6.;9.;99.];;
```

The preceding input produces the following output:

```
val it : int list = [6]
```

This means that the seventh element (`99` in this case) is anomalous as it doesn't match up with the other elements and is beyond the extreme ranges.

To find the ranges, the following call can be used:

```
getIQRRange [2.;3.;4.;5.;6.;9.;99.];;
```

This produces the following output:

```
val it : float * float = (-6.0, 18.0)
```

This means that extreme ranges are `-6` and `18`. So, any element that is less than -6 or greater than 18 will be tagged as anomalous. Thus, 99 is tagged as anomalous.

Detecting point anomalies using Grubb's test

Grubb's test (also known as the maximum normed residual test) is used to detect anomalies in a univariate dataset (which means there is only one variable per data instance) under the assumption that the data is generated by a Gaussian distribution. For each test instance x, its z score is computed as follows:

$$z = \frac{|x - \overline{x}|}{s}$$

Where $\overline{x}$ is the average of the data in the instances and s is the standard deviation of the data points.

The following functions determine the z scores of each element in the list:

```
let stdDevList list =
    let avg = List.average list
    sqrt (List.fold (fun acc elem -> acc + (float elem - avg) ** 2.0 ) 0.0 list
                        / float list.Length)

let zScores xs =
    let x_bar  = List.average xs
    let s = stdDevList xs
    let scores = xs |>List.map ( fun x -> abs (x - x_bar) / s )
    scores
```

A data instance is declared to be anomalous if it fulfills the following condition:

$$z > \frac{N-1}{\sqrt{N}} \sqrt{\frac{t^2_{\alpha/(2N),N-2}}{N-2+t^2_{\alpha/(2N),N-2}}}$$

Here, N is the number of elements in the collection and $t_{\alpha/(2N),N-2}$ is the threshold used to declare an instance to be anomalous or normal.

The following function finds the elements where the z score indicates that the element might be anomalous. The `xs` parameter denotes the entire collection and t denotes the value of $t_{\alpha/(2N),N-2}$.

```
let findAnomalies (xs:float list) t =
    let n = float xs.Length
    let threshold = (( n - 1.)/(sqrt  n)) * sqrt ( t ** 2. / ( n - 2. + t ** 2.))
    let z_scores = zScores xs
    xs |> List.mapi (fun i x -> if z_scores.[i] > threshold then i else - 1 )
       |> List.filter (fun z -> z <> -1)
```

The following code shows you how to use these functions to find anomalous data instances:

```
zScores [1.;100.;2.;4.5;2.55;70.]
findAnomalies [1.;100.;2.;4.5;2.55;70.] 0.89
```

The following lines produce the following output when run in F# interactive:

```
>
val it : float list =
  [0.7279145301; 1.756321212; 0.7028212398; 0.640088014; 0.6890199301;
   1.003522502]
>
val it : int list = [1; 5]
>
```

This means that the first and the last instances (100 and 70) are considered to be anomalous for the value of t set as 0.89.

Grubb's test for multivariate data using Mahalanobis distance

Grubb's test can be used for multivariate data by transforming multivariate data to univariate data using the following transformation:

$$y^2 = (x - \overline{x})' S^{-1} (x - \overline{x})$$

Where S is the covariance matrix of x.

The following code finds these y-squared values from a given x:

```
//Converting multivariate data to univariate data
//so that Grubb's test can be used.
let toUnivariate (xs:(float list)list) =
    let s = getCovarianceMatrix xs
    let x_bar = meanOf xs
    let mats = xs |> List.map (fun x -> (x, DenseMatrix.ofRowList[x] -
                                           DenseMatrix.ofRowList [x_bar]))
    mats |> List.map (fun elem -> (fst elem, (((snd elem) * s.Inverse()) *
                                    (snd elem).Transpose()).At(0,0)))
```

The following are the functions to calculate the covariance matrix:

```
#load "...\packages\MathNet.Numerics.FSharp.3.10.0\MathNet.Numerics.fsx"
open MathNet.Numerics.LinearAlgebra

//Returns the mean value of each column
let meanOf(x:(float list)list)=
    let k = x.[0].Length - 1
    let n = x.Length - 1
    let revs = [for i in 0 .. n -> [0 .. k] |> List.map(fun t -> x.[i].[t])]
    [0 .. k]|>List.map (fun k ->  List.average revs.[k])

//Gets the covariance matrix of the given matrix
let getCovarianceMatrix (x:(float list)list)=
    let n = x.Length //Number of rows
    let k = x.[0].Length//Number of columns
    let mean = meanOf(x)//Mean of the rows returns a vector of k elements
    //repmats is the repetition of mean row n times
    let repmats = DenseMatrix.ofRowList [for i in 0 .. n - 1 -> mean]
    let xC = (DenseMatrix.ofRowList x) - repmats
    let covMat = (xC.Transpose() * xC).DivideByThis(float n)
    covMat
```

The following is the input given:

```
let ys = toUnivariate [[2.;2.];[2.;5.];[6.;5.];[100.;345.]]
printfn "ys = %A" ys
```

This produces the following output:

```
ys = [([2.0; 2.0], -48066176.91); ([2.0; 5.0], -48066176.91);
 ([6.0; 5.0], -2584692.113); ([100.0; 345.0], -2.097348892e+12)]
```

Now, Grubb's test for univariate data can be applied on top of these generated values:

```
[-48066176.91; -48066176.91; -2584692.113; -2.097348892e+12]
```

The z scores of these values are:

```
[0.5773335755; 0.5773335755; 0.5773836562; 1.732050807]
```

As you can see, the z-score corresponding to the last entry is considerably bigger than the z-score of the rest. This means the last element in the multivariate dataset (which is [100;345]) is anomalous.

Imagine that these numbers in the random x variable denote the weekly spending of a person using a credit card. Using the aforementioned technique, we can find possible credit card fraud because fraud corresponds to anomalous entries. If a customer never spends more than $400 on a credit card in any given day of the week, then an expense of $9,000 is definitely an anomaly.

Code walkthrough

The covariance matrix is determined by the following equation, where x_k denotes the kth row of the multivariate data x. and $\hat{x}$ is the mean of entire multivariate data. $\hat{x}$ is denoted by `repmats` in the `getCovarianceMatrix` function.

$$\sum := \frac{1}{m}\sum_{k=1}^{m}(x_k - \hat{x})(x_k - \hat{x})^T$$

Thus $(x_k - \hat{x})$ is denoted by xC in the `getCovarianceMatrix` function.

Chi-squared statistic to determine anomalies

Ye and Chen used a χ^2 statistic to determine anomalies in the operating system call data. The training phase assumes that the normal data has a multivariate normal distribution. The value of the χ^2 statistic is determined as:

$$\chi^2 = \sum_{i=1}^{n}\frac{(X_i - E_i)^2}{E_i}$$

Where X_i denotes the observed value of the ith variable, E_i is the expected value of the ith variable (obtained from the training data), and n is the number of variables. A large value of χ^2 denotes that the observed sample contains anomalies.

The following function calculates the respective χ^2 values for all the elements in a collection:

```
let chiSquareStatistic xs es =
    List.zip xs es
      |> List.map (fun elem -> (fst elem,( (fst elem - snd elem ) ** 2.0)
                                                  /(fst elem)))
```

When this function is called with the same data `[1.;100.;2.;4.5;2.55;70.]` as the observed data and `[111.;100.;2.;4.5;2.55;710.]` as the expected values then the following result is obtained:

```
[(1.0, 12100.0); (100.0, 0.0); (2.0, 0.0); (4.5, 0.0); (2.55, 0.0);
   (70.0, 5851.428571)]
```

As you can see, the value of χ^2 is very high (121000.0 and 5851.428571) in the first and last observations. This means that the first and last observations are anomalous.

Detecting anomalies using density estimation

In general, normal elements are more common than anomalous entries in any system. So, if the probability of the occurrence of elements in a collection is modeled by the Gaussian or normal distribution, then we can conclude that the elements for which the estimated probability density is more than a predefined threshold are normal, and those for which the value is less than a predefined threshold are probably anomalies.

Let's say that x is a random variable of m rows. The following couple of formulae find the average and standard deviations for feature j, or, in other words, for all the elements of x in the *j*th column if x is represented as a matrix.

$$\mu_j = \frac{1}{m}\sum_{i=1}^{m} x_j^{(i)}$$

$$\sigma_j^2 = \frac{1}{m}\sum_{i=1}^{m}\left(x_j^{(i)} - \mu_j\right)^2$$

Given a new entry x, the following formula calculates the probability density estimation:

$$p(x)=\prod_{j=1}^{n} p\left(x_j;\mu_j,\sigma_j^2\right)=\prod_{j=1}^{n}\frac{1}{\sqrt{2\pi\sigma_j}}\exp\left(-\frac{\left(x_j-\mu_j\right)^2}{2\sigma_j^2}\right)$$

If $p(x)$ is less than a predefined threshold, then the entry is tagged to be anomalous, else it is tagged as normal.

The following code finds the average value of the jth feature:

```
//Calculates mu j
let mu(x:(float list)list)(j:int)=
    x |> List.map ( fun xrow -> xrow.[j])
      |> List.average

//The following function finds the square of the standard deviation
//of the jth feature: Calculates sigma squared j
let sigmaSqr(x:(float list)list)(j:int)=
     x |> List.map (fun xrow -> (xrow.[j] - mu x j) ** 2.0)
       |> List.average
```

```
//Calculates the product of the probabilities
//for each feature.
let px (trainingSet:(float list)list)(xtest:float list)=
    let n = trainingSet.Length
    let root2pi = sqrt ( 2.0 * 3.14159)

    let probs  = [for i in 0 .. n - 1 -> (1./root2pi * sqrt(sigmaSqr trainingSet i))
                                              (2.0 * sigmaSqr trainingSet i))]
    let mutable pxValue = 1.0
    probs |> List.map (fun z -> pxValue <- pxValue * z) |> ignore
    pxValue
```

Here is a sample run of the px method:

```
> let X = [[1.;3.;4.;5.];[3.;5.;6.;2.];[3.;5.;1.;9.];[11.;3.;3.;2.]];;

val X : float list list =
  [[1.0; 3.0; 4.0; 5.0]; [3.0; 5.0; 6.0; 2.0]; [3.0; 5.0; 1.0; 9.0];
```

```
  [11.0; 3.0; 3.0; 2.0]]

> let newX = [8.;11.;203.;11.];;

val newX : float list = [8.0; 11.0; 203.0; 11.0]

> px X newX;;
val it : float = 4.266413438e-16
>
```

Strategy to convert a collective anomaly to a point anomaly problem

A collective anomaly can be converted to a point anomaly problem and then solved using the techniques mentioned above. Each contextual anomaly can be represented as a point anomaly in N dimension where N is the size of the sliding window. Let's say that we have the following numbers: `1;45;1;3;54;1;45;24;5;23;5;5`. Then a sliding window of size 4 will produce the following series of collections can be generated by the following code

```
let data = [1;45;1;3;54;1;45;24;5;23;5;5]
let windowSize = 3
let series  = [for i in 0 .. data.Length-windowSize ->
                   data |> Seq.skip i |> Seq.take 3 |> Seq.toList]
```

This produces the following lists:

```
val data : int list = [1; 45; 1; 3; 54; 1; 45; 24; 5; 23; 5; 5]
val windowSize : int = 3
val indices : int list list =
  [[1; 45; 1]; [45; 1; 3]; [1; 3; 54]; [3; 54; 1]; [54; 1; 45];
   [1; 45; 24];[45; 24; 5]; [24; 5; 23]; [5; 23; 5]; [23; 5; 5]]
```

Now, as you have seen before, all of these lists can be represented as one point in three dimensions and Grubb's test for multivariate data.

Dealing with categorical data in collective anomalies

As an another illustrative example, consider a sequence of actions occurring in a computer, as shown below:

```
: : : http-web, buffer-overflow, http-web, http-web, smtp-mail, ftp,
http-web, ssh, smtp-
mail, http-web, ssh, buffer-overflow, ftp, http-web, ftp, smtp-mail,http-
web : : :
```

The highlighted sequence of events (`buffer-overflow`, `ssh`, `ftp`) corresponds to a typical, web-based attack by a remote machine followed by the copying of data from the host computer to a remote destination via `ftp`. It should be noted that this collection of events is an anomaly, but the individual events are not anomalies when they occur in other locations in the sequence.

These types of categorical data can be transformed into numeric data by assigning a particular number for each command. If the following mapping is applied to transform categorical data to numeric data:

Command	Numeric Representation
`http-web`	1
`ssh`	2
`buffer-overflow`	3
`ftp`	4
`smtp-mail`	5

Then the above series of commands will be a series of numbers like this. The numeric representation of the collective anomaly is the following:

```
: 1, 3, 1, 1, 5, 4, 1, 2, 4, 1, 2, 3, 4, 1, 4, 5, 1
```

These sequences can be processed by Grubb's test for identification of anomalous subsequences.

Summary

Anomaly detection is a very active field of research because what's anomalous now may not remain anomalous forever. This poses a significant challenge to designing a good anomaly detection algorithm. Although the algorithms discussed in this chapter mostly deal with point anomalies, they can be also used to detect sequential anomalies with a little bit of feature extraction.

Sometimes, anomaly detection is treated as a classification problem, and several classification algorithms such as k-NN, SVM, and Neural Networks are deployed to identify anomalous entries. The challenge, however, is to get well-labeled data. However, some heuristics are used to assign a score called the anomaly score to each data element, and then the top few with the highest anomaly scores (sometimes above a given threshold) are determined to be anomalous.

Anomaly detection has several applications, such as finding imposters using anomaly detection on keyboard dynamics, pedestrians, and landmine detection from images. Sometimes, anomaly detection algorithms are used to find novelties in articles.

Index

E

F

G

H

I

F# for Quantitative Finance

ISBN: 978-1-78216-462-3 Paperback: 286 pages

An introductory guide to utilizing F# for quantitative finance leveraging the .NET platform

1. Learn functional programming with an easy-to-follow combination of theory and tutorials.
2. Build a complete automated trading system with the help of code snippets.
3. Use F# Interactive to perform exploratory development.
4. Leverage the .NET platform and other existing tools from Microsoft using F#.

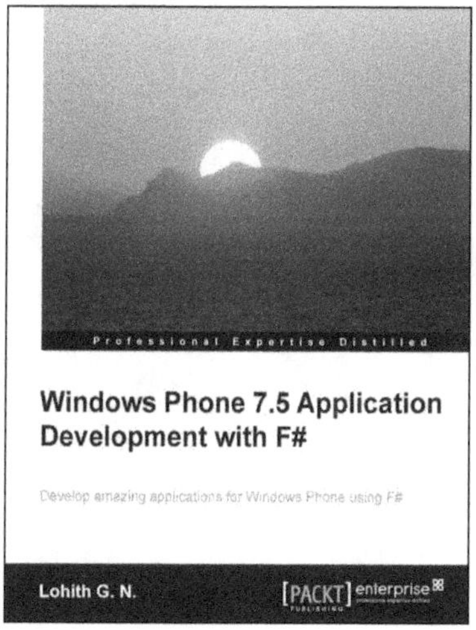

Windows Phone 7.5 Application Development with F#

ISBN: 978-1-84968-784-3 Paperback: 138 pages

Develop amazing applications for Windows Phone using F#

1. Understand the Windows Phone application development environment and F# as a language.
2. Discover how to work with Windows Phone controls using F#.
3. Learn how to work with gestures, navigation, and data access.

www.ingramcontent.com/pod-product-compliance
Lightning Source LLC
Chambersburg PA
CBHW060130060326
40690CB00018B/3816
* 9 7 8 1 7 8 3 9 8 9 3 4 8 *